tote
betting

the CHELTENHAM world of JUMP RACING

MICK FITZGERALD

with

SEAN MAGEE

CHELTENHAM
RACECOURSE
A JOCKEY CLUB RACECOURSE

RACING POST

This edition first published in Great Britain in 2010 by
Racing Post Books
High Street, Compton, Newbury, Berkshire, RG20 6NL

1 3 5 7 9 10 8 6 4 2

A catalogue record for this book is available from the British Library.

ISBN 978-1-905156-71-9

Typeset in Cheltenham typeface by SoapBox
www.soapboxcommunications.co.uk

Printed in the UK by Butler Tanner and Dennis Ltd, Frome

www.racingpost.com/shop

HALF-TITLE: Facing the Cheltenham hill.
FRONTISPIECE: Cheltenham Gold Cup day 2010 with, third from left in the middle tier, Her Majesty the Queen.

CONTENTS

FOREWORD

EDWARD GILLESPIE

Managing Director, Cheltenham Racecourse

There is a rhythm about the jump racing season that builds fresh excitement into a familiar framework. Mention the Charlie Hall or the Hennessy, and we instantly recognise crucial races as the season gathers momentum. Onto that established framework new names are added each year, beneath those which stretch back to the start of the modern era when sponsorship and television coverage thrust the exploits of Arkle into the living rooms of the nation.

Courses are spread right across Britain, allowing the entire population to feel involved and to follow their local champions to the big occasions. Even the largest training stables are invariably tucked behind a village, providing welcome employment, engagement of that community, and celebrations in the pub that go down in local folklore.

Skills have been honed over the decades; training surfaces and fitness levels of horses and jockeys have advanced out of all recognition. No longer do trainers need to wait in hope of rain for prospects of fast work to get started. By mid-October the horses and courses are prepared. Ready-to-run imports from France have added an irresistible attraction for owners. The big yards now have teams of horses for every underfoot condition.

Competition is more intense than ever, yet jump racing retains a camaraderie that is admired by commentators across all sport. Here you will see the stars congratulating each other when separated by a whisker, in victory or defeat.

Ultimately, the season is focussed on four extraordinary days at Cheltenham in March. More than 500 horses will be trained to the peak of their ability to compete around the natural amphitheatre at the foot of Cleeve Hill, with the Irish at the heart of the action both on and off the track. Then three weeks later the jump racing circus moves to Aintree, for a race with a history that defines the sport.

But it would be a mistake to think drama, excitement and laughter is confined to the big occasions, and you will find just as much entertainment on a Monday at a small track such as Plumpton, where the incomparable AP McCoy rode his 3,000th winner.

Nobody has more passion for jump racing than the jockeys, and Mick Fitzgerald – who had so many great Cheltenham moments, including Gold Cup glory – has moved seamlessly from booting home winners to describing what makes the experience so compelling.

We hope that the words and pictures on the pages that follow will help you share our passion.

PREFACE

OPPOSITE: Winning on Big Matt at Ascot in May 1995.

I've been lucky enough to live in the world of jump racing for my whole working life – from my first winner at Ludlow in December 1988 to the fall in the 2008 Grand National which brought my riding career to a premature end, and since then in the racing media.

Throughout that time I've had the good fortune to experience the incomparable buzz of the great race meetings – notably the Cheltenham Festival, where I was lucky enough to ride several winners, including See More Business in the 1999 Gold Cup – and to share that world with my fellow jockeys and the owners, trainers, stable staff and racing fans whose passion make jump racing the vibrant, compelling, irresistible sport that it is.

But it's not just about Cheltenham and Aintree and the big days. Jump racing has so many moods, and for the true devotee a wet afternoon at Sedgefield, Towcester or Roscommon has a magic all its own – and it is that variety which for me is at the core of its appeal.

So I've set out in this book to celebrate all aspects of jump racing, remembering the greats of the past – equine and human – and saluting the leading lights of the sport at the present time. With a golden generation of jump jockeys in action every day and the presence of wonderful horses like Kauto Star and Denman, we're living through an especially upbeat chapter in the story of jump racing, and now is the perfect time to show what the sport is all about.

In putting this book together I've worked closely with Sean Magee as editor and John Schwartz as designer, and I'd like to thank them – and Julian Brown and James de Wesselow at Racing Post Books – for all their efforts.

Welcome to my world.

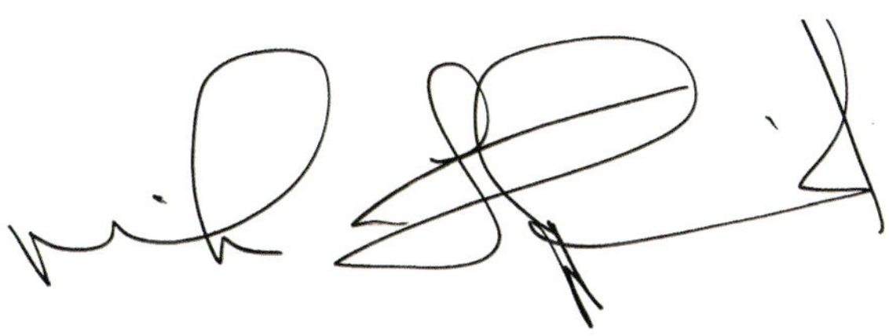

Networking
Solutions Ltd
14
3

THE JUMPING YEAR

PREVIOUS SPREAD: The field in the 2001 Whitbread Gold Cup at Sandown Park at the first open ditch, with winner Ad Hoc (Ruby Walsh, green cap) third from the right.

Jump racing these days is a sport for all seasons: the rising temperature of spring; the sun (sometimes) of summer; autumn bringing the rain which will ease the ground; the dark, soaked gloom of winter, when the last race or two seem to taking place in the dark; and then, as the Cheltenham Festival approaches, that invigorating whiff of spring in the air again.

Time was when the National Hunt season – as it was then known – in Britain would stage its last really big occasion on Whitbread Gold Cup day at Sandown Park in late April and then bump along quietly with a few small meetings until finishing at Stratford or Market Rasen in early June. All involved would then enjoy a couple of months' rest and relaxation before starting afresh, again with comparatively small meetings, in late July or early August.

Nowadays things are very different. After various fiddles with the beginning and end, the season goes out with a bang on the finale day at Sandown, and the new season starts the very next day.

Whether jump racing should be a round-the-calendar sport has been the subject of much debate over the years. From the jockey's perspective, when you're at the top of the tree you'd like to have a break, because jockeys – like footballers – can be carrying niggling injuries which detract from their performance, and in the days when there was a gap between seasons you could give these time to heal without feeling any pressure that you were missing out on the action.

But for some of the other lads, such as those associated with stables who tend to come good in the spring and summer months, they simply can't afford the luxury of having time off.

I loved taking a break, and in my last few years of riding I'd agree with my boss Nicky Henderson, who had few runners during the period of summer jumping, that I could have much of July and August off. I invariably felt better afterwards.

Modern turf management and watering technology have allowed certain courses to stage a programme of jump racing through the summer months when traditionally the ground would have been too firm for the sport, and many tracks have benefited from the change – notably Worcester, which is situated right on the banks of the River Severn and is liable to suffer very badly from waterlogging. (Worcester has attracted a good deal of criticism over some of its facilities, but from a jockey's point of view it's a great track to ride: very fair, with no traps. It's a mark of Worcester's quality that Morley Street won the Fred Rimell Memorial Novices' Chase there.)

Market Rasen stages the first really valuable race of the new season in the **Summer Plate,** run in mid-July, but it's not until the ground starts to ease with the onset of autumn that the season gets into full swing.

Full swing in Britain, that is – but in Ireland the **Galway Festival**, which now runs over seven days, tests the stamina of racegoers to the limit. (See page 148.)

Cheltenham, the sport's premier venue, provides many of the season's milestones, and the **Showcase** meeting in mid-October signals the return to action of some of those horses whose continuing participation is such an appealing aspect of jump racing. On the Flat, the very best horses tend to have meteoric careers, and the racing public is only getting to appreciate just how good they are when they are whisked off to stud. Sea The Stars, who carried all before him through his magnificent campaign in 2009 which culminated in that brilliant victory in the Prix de l'Arc de Triomphe, is a case in point. His sensational Arc win proclaimed him one of the greatest racehorses of all, but it was his last race. Contrast that brief – if dazzling – career with the longevity of horses like Kauto Star and Denman, who season after season return to action to delight their fans.

Local trainer Nigel Twiston-Davies has made a point of targeting horses at the valuable prizes on offer so early in the season at the Showcase, and has enjoyed prolific success at the meeting.

The Saturday of the Showcase meeting usually coincides with Champions' Day at Newmarket, the last really big fixture of the Flat season, when a star-studded programme features the Champion Stakes, Cesarewitch and Dewhurst Stakes – and thus the baton of top-class racing is passed from one racing code to the other.

A handful of the best staying chasers will return to action in the **Charlie Hall Chase** at Wetherby in late October, and though there is a long season ahead of them and they will be far from fully fit so early in the campaign, plenty of horses have won the Charlie Hall *en route* to bigger things later on. I won the Charlie Hall on See More Business twice. In 1999, the year he'd won the Gold Cup, he demolished the track record, and on his next outing won the

The 2008 Bet365 Charlie Hall Chase: winner State Of Play and Paul Moloney in full flight.

King George VI Chase at Kempton Park for the second time; and he hosed up in 2000. I won the race for a third time on Marlborough in 2002.

Early November brings the **Haldon Gold Cup** at Exeter, which over the last few years has become increasingly significant in seeing the reappearance of some top chasers. But the Haldon Gold Cup also has sad associations: it was in this race in 2005 that triple Gold Cup winner Best Mate dropped dead near the final fence after having been pulled up.

If the jumps season were an operatic *diva*, the early weeks of autumn would see her engaging in increasingly assured vocal exercises – and then bursting into full voice with the **Open Meeting** at Cheltenham in mid-November.

For the last few years the Friday of the Open Meeting has been designated 'Countryside Day', displaying Cheltenham's support for country issues. Feature race that day is the **Glenfarclas Cross-Country Chase** over just short of four miles.

Sunday's main race is the **Greatwood Handicap Hurdle**, but as far as the racing is concerned, top of the bill over the three days is Saturday's **Paddy Power Gold Cup**, a handicap chase over 2 miles 4½ furlongs and one of the most prestigious races of the season, which started life as the Mackeson Gold Cup back in 1960. The first seven runnings were over two miles, and produced some top-notch winners. In 1960 and 1962 the race was won by Tom Dreaper-trained Fortria, and the 1965 running went to the brilliant, barnstorming two-miler Dunkirk, who carried 12st 7lb. Dunkirk, who had a trail-blazing career before meeting a tragic end when killed taking on Arkle in the 1965 King George VI Chase, was an irrepressible front-runner, and I've always liked the reported reaction of Dave Dick, a real cavalier in an age of devil-may-care jump jockeys, after he had first ridden the horse in a race. Dunkirk

Both of us as neat as you like: See More Business winning the 2000 Peterhouse Group Charlie Hall Chase.

Imperial Commander and Paddy Brennan in autumn 2009: ABOVE, in total control beating the Queen's Barbers Shop in the Paddy Power Gold Cup at Cheltenham, and OPPOSITE, beaten by Ruby Walsh and Kauto Star by the narrowest margin imaginable in the Betfair Chase at Haydock Park – a story to be continued ...

had torn round in characteristic fashion, and as he dismounted Dave Dick said to trainer Peter Cazalet: 'Blimey!' That summed up this brilliant horse in a single word.

The distance of the Mackeson was increased to 2½ miles – or thereabouts in its present-day version – in 1967, and over the years has been landed by a succession of familiar horses, such as:

- **Gay Trip,** who won in 1969, and in 1970 won the Grand National over two miles further;
- **Bachelor's Hall** (1977), who went on to win both the Hennessy and the King George VI Chase that year:
- **Dublin Flyer,** one of the most popular chasers of the 1990s;
- and dual winners **Half Free** (1984 and 1985), **Bradbury Star** (1993 and 1994) and **Cyfor Malta** (1998 and 2002).

Added spice is brought to the Open Meeting with some strongly contested novice chases, for although the season is still young, the novice divisions will already be sorting themselves out, and this is the time to start identifying stars of the future. In the last few years many future stars have gone through their paces as novices at the Open: Best Mate, for example, won a novice chase at the meeting in 2000, and Denman did the same in 2006 (when the runner-up was subsequent Grand National winner Don't Push It).

It was less than twenty years ago that the November meeting at Aintree, home of the Grand National, was revived. There had been so many twists and turns in the story of the National course – how it was about to be sold for development in the 1970s and was then rescued – that simply keeping the National itself going had been a Herculean task, but as the racecourse facilities improved and the standard of racing at the Grand National meeting got better and better, the new-found confidence around the place led to the reinstatement of the traditional autumn meeting – and, to the great joy of all jumping fans, the revival of some of the old races over the National fences themselves.

FOLLOWING SPREAD: Jumps well – Sam Thomas, that is, in the 2008 ToteSuper7 Grand Sefton Chase, while his horse Gwanako peeks over from the other side of the Chair fence. Ahead of Sam, Graham Lee parts company with Regal Heights in more orthodox fashion.

3
totepool

The 2008 Totesport.com Becher Chase: Black Apalachi (Denis O'Regan) shows his liking for the Aintree fences: he went on to finish runner-up in the 2010 Grand National.

The contemporary version of the **Grand Sefton Chase** is run over 2 miles 5½ furlongs of the Grand National course, with the start near the Melling Road, on the approach to what is the second last fence in the National. Thus the Chair, one of the most fearsome of all the National fences, is the third fence – depending on your point of view, too early for comfort on a hard-pulling horse, or nice and early to get behind you.

The **Becher Chase** is run over 3¼ miles, starting immediately after Valentine's Brook, and like the Grand Sefton is a handicap. Naturally enough, the Becher Chase can be a good indicator of Grand National prospects: Black Apalachi, winner in 2008, finished runner-up to Don't Push it in the 2010 National.

Like the Paddy Power Gold Cup, Grand Sefton and Becher Chase, the **Hennessy Cognac Gold Cup** at Newbury in late November (sometimes early December) is a handicap, when the best horse in the field will not, at the weights, necessarily be the winner – and therefore the Hennessy is not strictly one of the unofficial 'Classics' of the jumps season, a badge which for staying chasers belongs only to the King George VI Chase at Kempton at Christmas and the Cheltenham Gold Cup in mid-March.

Yet for the jumping fraternity, professionals and racegoers alike, the Hennessy is indisputably one of the biggest races, not only of the season, but of jumping history. Every single jockey wants to have the Newbury showpiece on his cv, and it takes only the briefest glance over the roll of honour to see why. So many of the all-time greats have won it, and as the rider of one Hennessy winner I can assure you that it's a real privilege to have my name on that list.

First run at Cheltenham in 1957, the Hennessy Gold Cup was one of the valuable sponsored races which changed the profile of the sport in the late 1950s.

The first Hennessy was won by Mandarin, trained by Fulke Walwyn and owned by Madame Kilian Hennessy, whose family company of brandy distillers sponsored the race. The second – again at Cheltenham – went to Taxidermist, ridden by the amateur rider John Lawrence, who as John Oaksey was for decades one of the most popular racing pundits of all. (See page 235.) After three runnings at Cheltenham, the Hennessy moved to Newbury in 1960. (I have it on good authority that the reason the race was transferred from Prestbury Park to Newbury is that when, some time after the Hennessy sponsorship had been in place at Cheltenham, Mme Hennessy went into one of the racecourse bars for a glass of her family nectar, she discovered that the course was selling a rival brandy!)

Look at the names of some of the chasing stars who have won the Hennessy – among them Mandarin (twice), Mill House, Arkle

Familiar faces in the 1982 Hennessy Cognac Gold Cup: Night Nurse leads from the white-faced Corbiere, but the winner – not in picture – was Bregawn.

One of the great moments of my career – winning the 2005 Hennessy Cognac Gold Cup on Trabolgan (left), who at the last is inseparable from my old friend L'Ami, ridden by David Casey.

(twice), Spanish Steps, Diamond Edge, Bregawn, Burrough Hill Lad, One Man, Teeton Mill, Denman (twice) – and you'll immediately see why it's one of that handful of races which everyone in the sport wants to win.

It's the longest continuous sponsorship in racing, a race with a great history and a great durability. A few years ago, just as the gloom merchants were complaining that the Hennessy had lost some of its lustre, that it no longer attracted the *crème de la crème* of staying chasers, up popped Denman in 2007 to turn in an astonishing show of powerhouse jumping and relentless galloping under top weight to grind his rivals into the Berkshire mud – and then he went and did the same again in 2009.

OK, so Arkle, Mill House and the like are no longer around to warm the cockles on a winter afternoon, but there remains a real magic about the Hennessy, and I can't think of a better way of characterising it than by recalling how I felt after my one and only win in the race, on Trabolgan in 2005.

Outside my Cheltenham Festival winners and the Grand National on Rough Quest, it meant more than any other race I won. Why? Because of the race's history, yes, but also because it was a first Hennessy win not only for me, but also for Trabolgan's trainer Nicky Henderson, with whom I had enjoyed such a long association, and for his owner Trevor Hemmings, a lovely man whose passion is staying chasers. Indeed, 2005 was quite a year for Trevor. Trabolgan had given him his first Cheltenham Festival winner when we won the Royal & SunAlliance Chase, and then his wonderful horse Hedgehunter, trained in Ireland by Willie Mullins and ridden by Ruby Walsh, turned in a magisterial performance to win the Grand National. In addition, I was coming back from a bad injury at Hennessy time, and both Nicky and Trevor had shown faith in me when plenty of others would have been unconvinced that I was fit enough to ride the favourite in such a big race. No wonder I felt so emotional as I pulled up Trabolgan that I almost started crying.

To get a horse like Trabolgan to win a race of that stature took an immense amount of graft from a large number of people – the unsung stable staff as well as the higher-profile owner, trainer and jockey – and winning the Hennessy was for me the very essence of what makes jump racing such an amazing sport, of how it binds together so many different people with a common goal.

If the Hennessy is for staying chasers, the best two-mile chasers – the sprinters of steeplechasing – get their first top-grade race of the season in early December in the **Tingle Creek Chase** at Sandown Park, named after a famous two-mile chaser of the 1970s whose flamboyant jumping endeared him to the jumping fraternity. Just look at that photo overleaf: if anybody ever asks you whether horses 'enjoy' racing, there – in one sensational image of Tingle Creek jumping – is the answer.

FOLLOWING SPREAD: Tingle Creek – a breathtaking leap under David Mould at Stratford.

Two of the great two-mile chasers doing battle in the 2004 William Hill Tingle Creek Chase: winner Moscow Flyer (Barry Geraghty) leads Azertyuiop (Ruby Walsh).

For a jockey, there's no better buzz than to ride Sandown on a good jumper, and to go round there on a sensational one like Tingle Creek must have been an absolute dream.

The Tingle Creek is always run at a fierce pace and there's no margin for error, which explains why the list of past winners contains pretty well all the best two-milers of recent memory, including Waterloo Boy, Viking Flagship, Direct Route, Flagship Uberalles (who won it three times – and for three different trainers!), Moscow Flyer (who won twice), Twist Magic (another dual winner) and Master Minded. The 2004 race, when Moscow Flyer beat Azertyuiop, Well Chief and Cenkos, must rank as one of the most thrilling races in living memory.

The following year I rode Kauto Star to win the Tingle Creek for Paul Nicholls, as stable jockey Ruby Walsh was sidelined through injury. At that time Kauto was a five-year-old chaser making his rapid rise to the top rather than the superstar he was to become, and in the Tingle Creek he faced what appeared to be formidable opposition, including such old favourites as Ashley Brook, Oneway and Monkerhostin, who had beaten Kauto Star at more favourable weights in the Haldon Gold Cup. Ashley Brook didn't have the word 'restraint' in his dictionary, and set a pretty strong pace. I'd been told to hold Kauto up, but I didn't want to disrupt his rhythm, and he swept into the lead at the Railway Fences and round the final turn, took the last two fences brilliantly and cruised home for an easy win.

By early December the big occasions of the jump racing year are coming thick and fast, each week bringing a fresh consignment of big races.

For sheer concentration of quality, the December meeting at Cheltenham – now called the **International** – takes some beating. The big steeplechase of this two-day fixture, the **December Gold Cup** over 2 miles 5 furlongs, began life as the Massey-Ferguson Gold Cup back in 1963, and the following year Arkle put up an heroic performance to be narrowly beaten under the huge burden of 12st 10lb.

Given the nature of the race, it's a natural target for horses who have run in the Paddy Power Chase four weeks earlier, but it was not until 1988 that Pegwell Bay became the first horse to win both races in the same season, a feat emulated by the dashing grey Senor El Betrutti in 1997. Fifty Dollars More and Beau Ranger did the double in different seasons, as did Fondmort, whom I rode to win the Tripleprint Gold Cup in December 2002 and the Paddy Power Gold Cup in November 2003.

The reason why there have been so few winners of both races is obvious: winning one puts the horse up in the weights, making winning the other that bit more difficult. But every time I went out to ride Fondmort at Cheltenham I felt that I had 10lb up my sleeve, so good was he round there. Indeed, he was much better at Cheltenham than anywhere else; you could set your clock by his jumping there, and he seemed to be able to make ground in places where an ordinary horse would be losing it. I loved him to bits.

His 2002 Tripleprint Gold Cup was particularly notable for his unforgettable jump at the last fence, which he gave about eighteen inches' clearance. Jockeys talk of a horse 'coming up out of my hands' in the final stride before taking off, but Fondmort's extraordinary jump that day was unlike anything I ever experienced. It really felt as if I was up in the air for longer than I had ever been, before or since – it was as if he were taking part in a Puissance competition.

That Cheltenham meeting also features the **International Hurdle**, a race designed to bring together leading candidates for the Champion Hurdle three months later.

Fondmort winning the Tripleprint Gold Cup in December 2002: never have I jumped a final fence so high!

If the Cheltenham Festival in mid-March is the pinnacle of the jumping year, the undisputed high point of the season up to the turn of the year – the pivot of the season, if you like – is the **King George VI Chase** over three miles at Kempton Park on Boxing Day.

Boxing Day at Kempton Park is one of the great occasions of the racing year, and there's always a terrific buzz around the Sunbury-on-Thames course. For most racing fans, King George day is as much a part of Christmas as carols or the tree, a chance to blow away the cobwebs and clear the head after the excesses of the day before. And where better to do that than Kempton Park, where the King George is supported by the **Christmas Hurdle,** a natural stepping stone towards the Champion Hurdle, and by top-notch novice action?

Some people have the idea that, given the proliferation of important action on Boxing Day, jockeys pass a very frugal and parsimonious Christmas period, but that was never the case for me. When I was riding I always loved those few days: they offered the chance to have time off – increasingly rare in this time of year-round jumping action and Sunday racing – and to have a few beers with friends, from inside and outside the weighing room.

Nor did I feel the need for my Christmas dinner to consist of a quarter slice of turkey breast and a lettuce leaf. I would eat a proper Christmas dinner, though with less piled on my plate than many would consider appropriate, and I never spent the afternoon lying around snoring. When the clock struck 6pm it was as if someone had thrown a switch: Christmas festivities were done, and I'd started to concentrate on the work in hand on the following day.

The one great imponderable hanging over racing over the Christmas period is the weather, and it's a rare Boxing Day when not a single fixture is lost to the extremities of the climate. If you

Rooster Booster (Richard Johnson) winning the Victor Chandler Bula Hurdle at Cheltenham in December 2002. Three months later he won the Champion Hurdle.

hear early that, say, Kempton is off, you have to be prepared to get down to Wincanton or up to Wetherby at very little notice, for if the weather is bad at one course, it might be fine at another.

I feel especially sorry for the jockeys outside the front rank when the weather disturbs the Christmas programme, as for stable second jockeys and for the so-called 'journeymen' this period offers the rare chance to ride some top-class horses in good races at the lesser meetings, and it can be a hammer blow to your bank balance, as well as to your self-esteem, if those opportunities are lost.

First run in 1937, the King George has long been established as a championship event only one rung below the Cheltenham Gold Cup in prestige, but they are very different races, and good form in one does not necessarily transfer to the other. The King George is 2½ furlongs shorter than the Gold Cup; right-handed, while the Gold Cup is left-handed; and is run on a flat track, as opposed to the undulations of Cheltenham.

Yet the outstanding quality of the King George is attested by the list of horses who have won both these iconic races, and by the multiple winners:

The majesty of 'Himself' in action: Arkle (Pat Taaffe) winning the 1965 King George VI Chase. Just look how alert he is.

Florida Pearl (Adrian Maguire) beats Best Mate (AP McCoy) in the 2001 Pertemps King George VI Chase – allowing 'Mutley' Maguire to lay the ghost of Barton Bank unseating him when clear at the last in the 1994 race.

- **won King George and Gold Cup in same season**: Cottage Rake (1948-49), Limber Hill (1955-56), Saffron Tartan (1960-61), Arkle (1965-66), Desert Orchid (1988-89), Best Mate (2002-03), Kicking King (2004-05), Kauto Star (2006-07 and 2008-09);
- **won King George and Gold Cup in same year**: Cottage Rake (1948), Mill House (1963), Arkle (1965), Captain Christy (1974), Burrough Hill Lad (1984), Desert Orchid (1989), See More Business (1999), Best Mate (2002), Kicking King (2005, when the King George was run at Sandown Park), Kauto Star (2007 and 2009);
- **quadruple King George winners**: Desert Orchid (1986, 1988, 1989, 1990) and the only horse to have won four in consecutive years, Kauto Star (2006, 2007, 2008, 2009);
- **triple King George winner**: Wayward Lad (1982, 1983, 1985);
- **dual winners**: Halloween (1952, 1954), Mandarin (1957, 1959),

Pendil (1972, 1973), Captain Christy (1974, 1975), Silver Buck (1979, 1980), The Fellow (1991, 1992), One Man (the 1995 race run at Kempton in January 1996, and 1996), See More Business (1997, 1999), Kicking King (2004, 2005).

Naturally enough, given the history and status of the race, winning the 1999 running on See More Business was one of the highest points of my career. He was at the peak of his considerable powers, having won the Gold Cup the previous March, but I imagined that the record-breaking Charlie Hall win would have taken a fair deal out of him. Not a bit of it. Paul Nicholls had done an outstanding job to produce him in such fantastic condition on Boxing Day, and it was just like sitting on a completely fresh horse. He travelled miraculously well throughout the race, and four out I allowed myself a peep round to see how the others were going. I couldn't believe my eyes: those still in sight were labouring, while See More Business was still coasting along so easily that it was like having a quiet hack. He coasted home to win by 17 lengths from Go Ballistic, whom he'd beaten by one length in the Gold Cup. Just amazing.

Hard on the heels of the King George VI Chase comes another of the great steeplechases of the year, but one completely different in character from the Kempton showpiece. The **Welsh National**, run over a strength-sapping 3 miles 5½ furlongs at Chepstow between Christmas and New Year, can be a real slog., as two complete circuits round Chepstow's undulations are enough to get to the bottom of any horse.

The closest I came to winning the Welsh National was on the mare Fiddling The Facts, who failed by just half a length to reel in Kendal Cavalier in 1998, and I know from experience that riding in the race can be very hard work indeed. There's always a big field and usually the going is soft or worse, so you'd think that the

thing to do would be to drop your horse out and gradually make up ground in the later stages, but that seemed not to work, and I soon concluded that dropping out was quite the wrong tactic. You need to keep handy.

The Welsh National naturally comes into consideration when assessing the form for the Grand National itself some three months later, and several horses have won both Chepstow's biggest race and the Aintree original. Rag Trade won in 1976 (when the race was run in February) and then became the second of only two horses ever to beat Red Rum in the Grand National, while other winners of both races are Corbiere (Chepstow 1982, Aintree 1983), Earth Summit (Chepstow 1997, Aintree 1998), Bindaree (Aintree 2002, Chepstow 2003), and Silver Birch (Chepstow 2004, Aintree 2007).

Now these are proper jump racing conditions: a typically muddy finish to the Coral Welsh National as Bindaree (Carl Llewellyn, right) collars Sir Rembrandt (Andrew Thornton) in the 2003 running.

But the Welsh National is not a race for plodders. Burrough Hill Lad and Master Oats both won the Welsh National and Cheltenham Gold Cup (though Master Oats won the Welsh National at Newbury, as Chepstow was unraceable on the original date), and in 1991 Carvill's Hill put up a sensational performance under Peter Scudamore to grind his opponents into the mud, leading most of the way before crossing the line twenty lengths clear of subsequent Grand National winner Party Politics. An unbelievable performance.

Meanwhile, there is cracking good sport at the Christmas meeting at Leopardstown. Top of the bill is the **Lexus Chase,** a valuable prize which in recent years has been won by Gold Cup heroes Best Mate (2003) and Denman (2007) as well as by the remarkable Beef Or Salmon, who ran in the race six years running and won three times. He beat Colonel Braxton to win in 2002; finished third to Best Mate in 2003; beat Best Mate in 2004; beat War Of Attrition (who was to win the Gold Cup the following

The bleak midwinter: Hexham racecourse in January 2010.

March) in 2005; was runner-up to The Listener in 2006; and finished fourth behind Denman – beaten less than six lengths – in 2007. Beef Or Salmon was never seen at his best in England, where he took part in five consecutive runnings of the Gold Cup but was only once in the frame, when fourth behind Best Mate in 2004. Yet with conditions in his favour – that is, soft or heavy ground at Leopardstown – he was a wonderful horse.

The **New Year's Day** meeting at Cheltenham is the perfect way to forget another festive hangover and focus even more closely on the Festival, then some ten or eleven weeks away.

Big-race action resumes in the New Year with the **Victor Chandler Chase** over 2 miles 1 furlong at Ascot and the **Peter Marsh Chase** over three miles at Haydock Park, while a small but select field will contest the **Irish Champion Hurdle** at Leopardstown. Istabraq, who won the Champion Hurdle three times, went one better in the Irish equivalent, winning four times on the trot between 1998 and 2001.

Cheltenham's final pre-Festival meeting comes in late January, the one-day **Festival Trials Meeting**. The **Argento Chase** is a race firmly established as a final prep for those being primed to run in the Gold Cup, while the three-mile **Cleeve Hurdle** provides a Festival warm-up for World Hurdle hopefuls.

Early in February the Irish version of the **Hennessy Cognac Gold Cup** over three miles at Leopardstown sorts out a few more Gold Cup hopefuls. Florida Pearl, trained by Willie Mullins and one of the most popular horses of recent memory, on both sides of the Irish Sea, won this race a remarkable four times – in 1999, 2000, 2001 and at the age of twelve in 2004.

Meanwhile, in England the Festival preparations come to a head with the mid-February meeting at Newbury. Most valuable race at this fixture is the **Totesport Trophy**, which started life as the Schweppes Gold Trophy back in 1963 at Liverpool before moving to Newbury the following year. It must be very annoying for the Tote, who have been sponsoring the race since 1987, that so many old racegoers still refer to the race as 'the Schweppes', but under the Tote's care this hugely competitive contest has become the most richly endowed handicap hurdle in Europe.

One of the great sights of jump racing: the Totesport Trophy field spread across the Newbury straight.

I was lucky enough to win the Tote Gold Trophy (as it was then called) three times in four years, all on horses trained by Nicky Henderson: Sharpical in 1998, Geos in 2000, and Landing Light in 2001. (Geos was a well fancied 15-2 chance when I won on him, but when he repeated the feat at 16-1 in 2004 he had Marcus Foley in the saddle, as I had smashed my arm at Sandown the previous week.)

It is always a tough race to ride in. A big field going lickety-split means precious little room to see what you're doing, and you have to be very aware of what might be going on around you, but Newbury is such a great track, roomy and inviting, that there are few genuine hard-luck stories. You need a horse with a bit of nous about him, and you need luck – or at least the avoidance of bad luck – in running.

The same Newbury programme has the **Aon Chase** over three miles, which Denman won before landing the 2008 Gold Cup and in which he unshipped AP at the third last in 2010, and the **Game Spirit Chase**, named in memory of one of the late Queen Mother's most popular horses and a standard prep race for the Queen Mother Champion Chase at the Festival.

The next major race is the **Racing Post Chase** at Kempton Park in late February, one of the most hotly contested three-mile handicap

chases of the season and a race which in previous incarnations had been won by greats like Easter Hero (1928), Crisp (1972) and Pendil (1973 and 1974). Desert Orchid won this under Richard Dunwoody in 1990, putting up what was regarded as one of his finest performances of all when carrying 12st 3lb and beating Delius by eight lengths after yet another stunning display of front-running and spring-heeled jumping.

A sadder memory is of Gloria Victis, the hugely promising Martin Pipe-trained chaser whose brilliant victory in the 2000 Racing Post Chase put him on the path to the Cheltenham Gold Cup, where he was fatally injured when still in contention at the second last.

And a bad personal memory: Rough Quest, on whom I won the

One that got away: Kelami (right) and I are beaten by Ruby Walsh on Gungadu in the 2008 Racing Post Chase.

1996 Grand National, had won the Racing Post Chase that season, ridden by Richard Dunwoody as I was claimed to ride the Nicky Henderson runner Amtrak Express – who unseated me at the last open ditch.

The Racing Post Chase card also has serious Festival prep races in the **Adonis Juvenile Novices' Hurdle** for four-year-olds with the **Triumph Hurdle** on the agenda, the **Dovecote Novices' Hurdle**, and the **Pendil Novices' Chase.**

With the Cheltenham Festival then so close, there's a bit of a lull in the sequence of high-class competition before all hell breaks loose at the foot of Cleeve Hill. And if the weather has interfered with Cheltenham preparations and caused meetings to be cancelled, some Festival hopefuls will still be scrabbling for a prep race as the end of February approaches, and not always with the expected result. In 2010 Zaynar, winner of the 2009 Triumph Hurdle and as yet unbeaten, was sent by Nicky Henderson all the way to the Border Country for what looked a pre-Champion Hurdle shoo-in in the Morebattle Hurdle at Kelso. The grey started at 1-14 but struggled in the very soft going and was beaten a length by Quwetwo, a result which gave Zaynar the dubious distinction of being the joint-shortest-priced loser in jump racing history. (To be fair to the horse, he ran a blinder in the Champion Hurdle itself, finishing an excellent third behind stable companion Binocular.)

Late February also brings the four-mile **Eider Chase** at Newcastle, usually considered an ideal preliminary to the Grand National (Comply Or Die won both races in 2008), and in early March, on the weekend immediately before the Festival, there's the **Imperial Cup,** the historic two-mile handicap hurdle run at Sandown Park.

So many months of preparation, for humans and horses alike, and then you wake up on Tuesday morning and it's the opening day of the **Cheltenham Festival** – which I'll look at in detail in the next section of the book.

It's hard to avoid a sense of anti-climax after the Festival has ended, but big-race action continues the following day with the **Midlands Grand National** over 4 miles 1½ furlongs at Uttoxeter.

Like the Welsh National, this race tends to be a real slog, but unlike that race it is rarely contested by a truly top-notch horse like Carvill's Hill or Master Oats. As at Chepstow, round Uttoxeter you cannot afford to be too far off the pace. It rides like a really tight course and there's little room for manoeuvre, with the result that the Midlands National is often a rough race.

Before we know it, in early April we're into the next big Festival of jump racing, the three-day **Grand National Festival** at Aintree.

BELOW AND OPPOSITE: The Luscious Ladies of Liverpool.

The Grand National itself is an event big enough to have its own section in this book, but each day of the meeting has a tremendous buzz – and not just on the racecourse itself. On all three days, and especially for 'Ladies' Day' on the Friday, the girls of Liverpool turn out in their finest attire – often, it seems, with the aim of wearing as little as the bounds of decency will allow. This is early April and the weather can be extremely changeable, but the Ladies of Liverpool defy the elements with a spirit and determination wondrous to behold. I remember that a few years ago the Friday brought a combination of freezing temperatures, hurricane-strength wind and steady rain, and yet the Bikini Competition was still oversubscribed. Those girls – and their guys – know how to enjoy themselves to the full, and the increasing involvement of the locals produces plenty of fine sights and is one of the big factors in how the Grand National meeting has grown in the last few years.

The Grand National jockeys annually doff their caps to the Liverpool ladies in their indescribable splendour, who regardless of conditions make those three days a never-ending and never-to-

be-forgotten fashion parade. Somebody must have told them that they won't need a coat, and that the way to combat cold and wet is the rapid and regular ingestion of alcohol. Whatever their tipple of choice, they add such a great buzz to what from the racing standpoint is already a fantastic meeting in its own right.

Young Kenny and Brendan Powell showing how it's done, on the way to landing the 1999 Marstons Pedigree Midlands Grand National.

Oh yes, the racing …

Thursday's card features the **Totesport Bowl**, a Grade 1 chase so often one outing too many for the reigning Cheltenham Gold Cup winner: Dawn Run fell at the first in 1986, Desert Orchid took a tumble in 1989, Kauto Star was beaten in 2008, Imperial Commander unseated Paddy Brennan in 2010.

The **Melling Chase** over 2½ miles on the Friday has seen some amazing finishes over the years, none more so than the 1995 race when Viking Flagship, Martha's Son and Deep Sensation – all winners of the Queen Mother Champion Chase in their time – came to the last fence locked together. It was only after a roof-raising battle up the run-in that Viking Flagship, as brave a horse as you could ask for, managed to get his head in front and win by a short head from Deep Sensation, with Martha's Son a length back in third. Many seasoned racing fans think that, outside Cheltenham and the National, this was as good a steeplechase as they've ever seen.

Saturday's card is dominated by the Grand National, but the top hurdlers get a look in with the **Aintree Hurdle** over 2½ miles, which

makes it a less than straightforward proposition for horses who have run prominently in the Champion Hurdle over nearly half a mile shorter. This race has produced some astonishing climaxes, notably the dead heat between Night Nurse and Monksfield in 1977 – the race before Red Rum won his third Grand National – and the battle in the mud between Charlie Swan on Istabraq and AP McCoy on Pridwell in 1998: Pridwell won by a head after a protracted battle from the last, and AP still considers that the best ride he ever gave a horse – and I'm not going to argue with that.

Just as Cheltenham's first meeting of the season coincides with Newmarket's last major meeting on the Flat, so its final meeting in April usually overlaps with the Craven Meeting at Newmarket, when the Flat steps up a gear as Classic hopefuls take the stage. The baton is being handed back, but there's still plenty of life in the jumps season.

The 4 miles 110 yards **Scottish Grand National** is the highlight of the jumping year at Ayr, and another of those intriguing and competitive handicaps which the racegoing public adore. Nearly

OPPOSITE: Two of the greatest ever finishes – at Aintree or anywhere else: Monksfield (Dessie Hughes, left) and Night Nurse (Paddy Broderick) at the last flight before dead-heating in the Templegate Hurdle in 1977; and (left to right) Martha's Son (Rodney Farrant), the winner Viking Flagship (Adrian Maguire) and Deep Sensation (Norman Williamson) at the last in the Mumm Melling Chase in 1995.

At full stretch: winner Grey Abbey (Graham Lee) and First Gold (AP McCoy) in the Betfair Bowl, 2005.

8
9

POWERS GOLD LABEL

Adrian Maguire and Baronet on the way to winning the Stakis Casinos Scottish Grand National in 1998.

PREVIOUS SPREAD: The first fence in the 2006 Irish Grand National at Fairyhouse.

three complete circuits of Ayr make the Scottish National a great spectacle, and it's been won by some famous horses – none more so than Red Rum, who in 1974 won it just two weeks after his second victory in the Aintree original. Since then both races have been won by Little Polveir and Earth Summit (who also won the Welsh National, making him the only horse ever to have won all three national Nationals in Britain).

I never won the Scottish National – the closest I came was second on Ad Hoc in 2001 – but it always struck me that the ideal horse for this race is one with a nice high cruising speed. Beyond that, you have to be wary of any runner for whom this gruelling race might be considered an afterthought at the end of a long hard season. Better to look for a horse who has noticeably been holding his form, or for one who has been specifically aimed at this race.

The **Punchestown Festival,** described on pages 145–8, occurs in late April or early May, while the same period sees the end of the jumps season in Britain with the finale day at Sandown Park, with the **Bet365 Gold Cup** the main attraction.

In its original incarnation as the Whitbread Gold Cup, this was initially run in 1957, the first of the handsomely sponsored steeplechases whose injection of support transformed the sport at a time when jump racing was becoming more and more popular through the medium of television. The Whitbread was soon followed by the Hennessy, the Mackeson and a succession of other commercially supported races – some of which survive, some of which don't – and as the Bet365 Gold Cup remains one of the most popular races of the season. It usually attracts a large field, the sight of which streaming over the fences down Sandown's back straight is invariably uplifting; it contains a good many of the most popular chasers in training – like dear old Monkerhostin, who won at the age of eleven in 2008; and as a handicap it's a great betting medium.

Early on in the 1984 Whitbread Gold Cup: left to right, Diamond Edge, Polar Express and last-gasp winner Special Cargo.

As with so many of these famous races, the briefest glance at the list of past winners is all you need for an affirmation of what makes it special: Arkle won in 1965, Mill House in 1967, The Dikler in 1974, Desert Orchid in 1988 …

And the 1984 running produced what so many consider the most exciting steeplechase ever run: Diamond Edge, going for his third win in the race at the age of thirteen, was locked in a pulsating battle with Lettoch and Plundering up the hill from the last fence when – zoom! – up the outside flew the Queen Mother's grand old servant Special Cargo, ridden by Kevin Mooney to beat the lot of them. A finish of two short heads – and John Oaksey on Channel 4 Racing was spot on when he declared, 'I honestly have never seen a finish as exciting as this.'

That's what this race can produce: the very best of jump racing in a superlative arena, with a committed crowd – winning or losing – cheering the runners home. No wonder that the Sandown afternoon is now firmly established as the perfect way to end the jumps season.

And the very next day, it all begins again.

PADDY POWER
Paddy Power
Smurfit Kappa Group
ORDER MERIT
SPINAL RESEARCH
Irish Independent
William HILL.com
Smurfit Kappa Group
Smurfit Kappa Champion Hurdle

THE CHELTENHAM FESTIVAL

PREVIOUS SPREAD: The Cheltenham Festival 2010 – (BELOW) by Royal Appointment.

CHELTENHAM is a magical place, and every year, whatever the results, the Festival is an unforgettable occasion. The racing is of the highest quality, and with so many thousands of Irish racing fans pouring into Prestbury Park for the week, so is the *craic*. There's simply nothing like it.

I can trace my love of the place to the minute, to the moment when Dawn Run and Jonjo O'Neill climbed the hill for that incredible last-gasp win in the 1986 Gold Cup, the one and only horse to have won both the Champion Hurdle and the Gold Cup. I was fifteen at the time, watching on television at Richard Lister's yard in Coolgreany – the month before I had my first race ride in public – and seeing the mare's amazing rally to collar Wayward Lad, and the tumultuous reaction of the crowd to her victory, sent the hairs on my neck standing up. All Ireland stopped to applaud the achievement of this marvellous horse and her never-say-die jockey, and that's when the fire was ignited within me: I had to ride a winner at Cheltenham, and even beyond that, I had to ride the winner of the Gold Cup. My life would not be complete until I had done it.

In the event, it was not until March 1992 that I first rode at the Festival, on a 25-1 shot named Crystal Heights in the Coral Golden Hurdle. Even though I was strictly a bit-part player that day, a 3-pound claiming Irish jockey scarcely known in Britain, I sensed the buzz, the air of fevered anticipation about the whole place the instant I walked into the course. It just seemed such a wonderful place to be, with a huge range of people all united in one purpose, to have a winner at Cheltenham – and having a role in the action, however humble, was very special indeed.

The weighing room had a completely different mood from any other day's racing – even Grand National day – and that sense of being part of an extra-special occasion never left me, no matter how many years I went back there or how many winners I was privileged to ride.

Cheltenham magic – the roar as the field for the first race of the meeting comes up to the stands.

In the changing room you'd see people you didn't often see – like jockeys from Ireland or France or even further afield – so some of the guys you knew, and some you didn't. You'd feel yourself looking at people out of the corner of your eye, but not giving anything away.

From the racing point of view, a large part of what makes Cheltenham so special is that every race is the race of the season in its category – two-mile chase, three-mile hurdle, whatever – which makes every event so amazingly competitive. And from the jockey's point of view, there is no part of any race there when, as on other tracks, you can get a little breather into your horse and calm down before the final effort. Everyone is trying their utmost. It's almost invariably a case of being flat out from the start, and everything feels likes it's happening at a much faster pace than usual.

When you're on the right horse, everything you do falls into place. You feel that you can't fail, and for me there was no greater feeling

in the world than turning for home at Cheltenham, looking around at the other horses still in contention and thinking: I've got these covered!

But still you can't take your eye off the ball. It's a long way home from the turn in, and there are obstacles to jump in the straight and then that grinding hill up to the winning post. When you clear the last, and you sense the other horses tying up around you, you hear a noise that you only ever hear at Cheltenham. It pours down in waves from both sides of the track as you make that aching climb – BANG! BANG! BANG! BANG!, like masses of people beating drums.

I've never heard anything like it, but that's not the end of the Cheltenham experience for a jockey.

Over the years the course management has taken all sorts of measures not only to improve the facilities for racegoers, but to enhance the sheer theatre of the place. This is nowhere better illustrated than the walk in front of the stands that all the finishers take from the racecourse back to the winner's enclosure and unsaddling area. If you've ridden the winner, the roars of appreciation which roll off the stands towards you as you come back are just amazing, and it doesn't matter whether you've won on a heavily backed favourite or a rank outsider. The Cheltenham crowd is so enthusiastic, and so appreciative of what any horse and jockey need to do to win a race at the Festival, that even less fancied winners get a huge ovation. Cheltenham people always appreciate what they've just seen, whether they've backed the winner or not.

And not only the winners get an ovation. Think of the roar that greeted Kauto Star when Ruby Walsh had hacked him back after his crashing fall in the 2010 Gold Cup. Kauto Star was a beaten favourite, but the crowd's relief in seeing that he and Ruby were both in one piece and ready to fight another day spoke volumes about the spirit of Cheltenham.

I wonder where this lot are from …

OPPOSITE: Enda Bolger's team at their early-morning survey of the cross-country course.

THE COURSE

A major part of the magic of Cheltenham is the racecourse itself. Open and spacious, with beautifully made and invitingly wide fences, it is a joy to ride on.

There are two separate circuits (plus the cross-country course in the middle), and before changes brought in for the 2010-11 season the simplest way to identify which course was in use was that in a steeplechase on the Old Course there was one jump in the straight, whereas in a chase on the New Course there were two. The changes mean that there are now two fences in the straight on both courses.

The official form book describes both courses as follows: 'Left-handed, galloping, undulating and testing track with stiff fences,' but I'd take issue with the word 'galloping'. While each course presents

Tuesday morning, 7.30am: Ferdy Murphy's string head for the gallops in the centre of the course.

its own challenge to a jockey, as far as I'm concerned neither is a galloping track. Riding in a race at Cheltenham – and especially in a hurdle over the Old Course – it feels like you're spending most of the time on the turn, rather than letting your horse stride out over long stretches of straight. You need a horse which can jump at speed as well as hold his position through the race.

A textbook example of this was the performance of Dunguib in the Spinal Research Supreme Novices' Hurdle, opening race of the 2010 Cheltenham Festival. Trained in Ireland by Philip Fenton and winner of the Weatherbys Champion Bumper in 2009, he was the banker of the 2010 meeting for so many punters – and a stone-cold certainty for a good many more. Indeed, he was so highly regarded that the run-up to the Festival had seen an animated debate about whether he should miss the novices' race in favour of the Champion Hurdle itself.

He went for the Supreme Novices' Hurdle, and what happened? He was travelling well enough when an error at the fourth last hurdle caused him to lose his place. All of a sudden he found himself in a position he didn't want to occupy, and while in a lesser race he might have been able to make up the deficit without too much fuss, at that level the pace is such that all the good horses ahead of him were getting away from him, and trying to make ground at that pace on the downhill run towards the straight was, not surprisingly, beyond him. He finished fourth, and many punters spent the rest of the meeting trying to claw back their Dunguib losses.

The simple lesson for riding round Cheltenham is: Be on a horse that jumps well, travels well and is able to hold his position. Given the speed of most races round there, if you have to think about going for a gap, you're too late and it will have been taken by someone else. And so you have to put yourself in the right place all the time in order to be ready to fill those holes as they occur.

On both the Old Course and the New, much is made of the difficulty of the obstacles on the run down to the home straight.

High winds brought abandonment of the Wednesday card in 2008 – resulting in ten races on Thursday and nine on Friday. A masterpiece of reorganisation.

FOLLOWING SPREAD: Which way? The New Course is on the left, the Old on the right.

GUINNESS GUINNESS
Paddy Power
totesport
GUINNESS GUINNESS
8

Wragge&Co

Foot and mouth disease caused cancellation of the 2001 Festival.

Naturally a fence is potentially more hazardous than a hurdle, but over hurdles on the Old Course it is important to jump the second last well or you run the risk of being pushed too far wide and losing vital ground as you swing towards the straight.

In a steeplechase on the Old Course, one of the bogey fences was the third last, the first on the downhill stretch, although it has been modified in recent years and doesn't have as many fallers as before. My fall on Remittance Man in the 1994 Queen Mother Champion Chase – which at the time I thought was going to bring a premature end to my infant career as Nicky Henderson's stable jockey – was typical of what could happen at that fence.

Back then it was a brutal fence. At that stage of the race the taps were turned on and there was absolutely no margin for error. By seeing too ambitious a stride for Remittance Man I was asking him an impossible question, and I got found out. One positive to come out of that incident – and boy, did I need a positive that day! – was that I learned more from that one fall than from any other ride in my career, and the lesson was this: it doesn't matter how much you want a horse to jump an obstacle, if he hasn't got the momentum or the petrol in the tank to come up on the stride you're asking him for, he isn't going to make that jump.

On the Old Course before the changes, that lesson regarding the third last also applied at the second last. If you needed your horse to come up for you but you weren't holding your position, you'd end up on the floor. The ground fell away on the landing side, and unless you got it right, gravity would take over and your horse would fall.

On the New Course I used to think that the fourth from home – where Kauto Star took that crashing fall in the 2010 Gold Cup – was the worst fence. As with the third last on the Old Course, it's a critical juncture in a race, and there's no margin for error.

Over hurdles, the New Course is much stiffer than the Old, with only two hurdles in the last seven furlongs or so. That's why on that course you need a hurdler that can really stay. But whether you've reached the last by way of the Old Course or New, Cheltenham's final challenge is the most taxing of all: the hill.

It's a basic theme in any talk about Cheltenham that the hill tests the resolve and guts of horses to the hilt, but to get a true sense of the incline, you have to go and stand at the turn into the straight. Television gives the impression of how tough the hill is, but only by standing at the foot of it and looking up towards the winning post will you understand its demands. No wonder so many horses who look to be certain winners at the final fence or final flight don't make it. If you can't get up the Cheltenham hill, you won't win.

But the challenges which the course presents are appropriate for a venue which brings together in competition the very best horses, jockeys and trainers in the sport. Challenge is what Cheltenham is all about.

The 2010 Glenfarclas Cross-Country Chase: Heads Onthe Ground (Paul Carberry, red cap) shares the lead with 2007 Grand National winner Silver Birch (Robbie Power). The winner A New Story (Adrian Heskin) is on the extreme left, and runner-up L'Ami (John Thomas McNamara) on the extreme right; the grey Lacdoudal (Rhys Flint, second left), finished third.

THE RACES

OPPOSITE: A dream come true: Paddy Brennan and Imperial Commander return after winning the 2010 Totesport Cheltenham Gold Cup. I'm in the background on the right (working with John Inverdale for Radio 5 Live), wearing headphones and trying not to look green with envy.

Every single race at the Cheltenham Festival is a major contest in its own division, but the two really big races in terms of history and public awareness – the two whose result will be mentioned on the television news that evening, if you like – are the Gold Cup and Champion Hurdle.

CHELTENHAM GOLD CUP

The Gold Cup, a steeplechase run over 3 miles 2½ furlongs of the New Course on the final day of the meeting, is quite simply the Holy Grail of jump racing. The Grand National is a uniquely challenging race and a thrilling contest in which to ride – some of you may remember my often quoted reaction to winning it on Rough Quest in 1996! – but the Gold Cup at Cheltenham is for the very best staying chasers of a generation, and the one race which every child who dreams of becoming a jump jockey is desperate to win.

While the Grand National is a handicap designed to bring the chances of all the runners together, the Gold Cup is run at level weights (though mares get an allowance), so almost invariably it is won by the very best horse on the day.

You only have to cast an eye down the Gold Cup roll of honour and the case for its place at the pinnacle of the sport is made:

- **Easter Hero**, outstanding winner in 1929 and 1930;
- **Golden Miller,** who won the race five times between 1932 and 1936;
- **Prince Regent**, brilliant Irish-trained winner in 1946;
- **Cottage Rake**, triple winner trained by Vincent O'Brien to win in 1948, 1949 and 1950;

Golden Miller and his doting owner Dorothy Paget.

- **Mandarin**, the little horse who won in 1962;
- **Mill House**, 'The Big Horse' who powered home in 1963;
- **Arkle**, the immortal 'Himself' who won in 1964, 1965 and 1966;
- **L'Escargot**, dual winner in 1970 and 1971;
- **The Dikler,** who ran in the race seven years in a row and beat Pendil a short head to win in 1973;
- **Dawn Run**, who in 1986 became the only horse ever to win the Champion Hurdle and Gold Cup;
- **Desert Orchid,** who overcame all sorts of adversity to win in 1989;
- **The Fellow,** winner at the fourth attempt in 1994, after having twice been short-headed in the race;
- **Best Mate**, triple winner in 2002, 2003 and 2004;
- **Denman**, who pulverised the opposition in 2008;
- **Kauto Star**, in 2007 and 2009, the only horse ever to regain the Gold Cup title;
- **Imperial Commander,** who gatecrashed the Kauto v. Denman showdown in 2010 to provide a local winner.

Not quite eminent enough to claim a place on that list of Gold Cup Greats is See More Business, but he's very special to me, as he gave me the highest point of my riding career when winning in 1999 – and I can still remember every stride.

The two market leaders were Florida Pearl, ridden by Richard Dunwoody and the latest in a long line of Irish-trained chasers to have been dubbed 'The New Arkle', and the Venetia Williams-trained grey Teeton Mill, who was unbeaten in four outings that season, including the Hennessy Gold Cup and King George VI Chase. See More Business, who had won the King George VI Chase ridden by Andrew Thornton in 1997, had run poorly in the Kempton race on Boxing Day 1998 and was allowed to start at 16-1 at Cheltenham. The previous year, when he was desperately unlucky to be carried out by the lame Cyborgo early on in the race, he had started 11-2 second favourite. But punters have short memories, and plenty must have been kicking themselves as we reached the top of the hill second time round in the Gold Cup. Teeton Mill had been pulled up on the first circuit, and all the better-fancied horses except Florida Pearl had faded away as See More Business and 66-1 chance Go Ballistic turned down the hill for the final time.

See More Business had travelled beautifully throughout the race and jumped well – with the exception of a mistake at the fence in front of the stands at the end of the first circuit – and I was beginning to get confident. For a moment going down the hill we seemed to be outpaced by Go Ballistic, but then I saw Richard starting to get to work on Florida Pearl, and I knew that the threat from that quarter was diminishing.

About to achieve a lifetime's ambition, as See More Business (left) jumps the last in the 1999 Tote Cheltenham Gold Cup alongside Go Ballistic (Tony Dobbin).

We turned for home in full flight, and although Go Ballistic still had the lead, I had ridden that horse before and knew that See More Business would outstay him. We were a length down at the second last, but as far as I was concerned those last two fences were as good as not there: I knew we were going to meet them running and take them cleanly, and we did. Go Ballistic and See More Business touched down as one at the last, and away we went up the hill, with See More Business digging deep – and we won by a length, with Florida Pearl way back in third.

It was a fantastic feeling – a lifetime's ambition fulfilled – and even now I cannot properly put into words just how winning the Gold Cup felt. But more than anything, I remember how See More Business pulled up in a matter of seven or eight strides after crossing the line, and walked back past the packed stands with his head bowed. He'd given his all, and giving your all is what you do at the Cheltenham Festival.

The sensational 1990 Tote Cheltenham Gold Cup: 100-1 winner Norton's Coin (no. 7), ridden by the great Graham McCourt, at the last with Toby Tobias (Mark Pitman).

CHAMPION HURDLE

As the Gold Cup is the annual championship race for staying steeplechasers, so the Champion Hurdle is the summit to which all hurdlers aspire. It's invariably an intensely competitive race and a great spectacle.

Run over 2 miles 110 yards on the Old Course on the opening day of the Festival, the Champion Hurdle has a history hardly less vibrant than that of its chasing equivalent – though for me it was the one that got away, as third on Blue Royal behind the great Istabraq in 2000 was the closest I got. (In 2009, at the first Festival after I had retired from the saddle, the Champion Hurdle was won by Punjabi, a horse I would probably have ridden as stable jockey to Nicky Henderson.)

Just as the special nature of the Gold Cup is declared by the roll-call of great winners, so it is with the Champion Hurdle. There have been five triple winners:

A true great: Istabraq (Charlie Swan) with myself on Blue Royal at the final flight of the Smurfit Champion Hurdle in 2000. Blue Royal was beaten a neck for second by Hors La Loi III.

bgc
1
Smurfit Kappa Group
4

Nearly man: Theatreworld, trained by Aidan O'Brien to finish runner-up in three consecutive Champion Hurdles: to Make A Stand in 1997 and to Istabraq in 1998 and 1999.

- **Hatton's Grace** (1949, 1950, 1951);
- **Sir Ken** (1952, 1953, 1954);
- **Persian War** (1968, 1969, 1970);
- **See You Then** (1985, 1986, 1987);
- **Istabraq** (1998, 1999, 2000);

and eight dual winners:

- **Insurance** (1932, 1933);
- **National Spirit** (1947, 1948);
- **Bula** (1971, 1972);
- **Comedy Of Errors** (1973, 1975);
- **Night Nurse** (1976, 1977);
- **Monksfield** (1978, 1979);
- **Sea Pigeon** (1980, 1981);
- **Hardy Eustace** (2004, 2005).

The key requirement in a Champion Hurdle winner is the ability to jump cleanly at speed. To some observers, hurdles take significantly less jumping than steeplechase fences, but jumping ability is an absolute must for a top-class hurdler, and so many of the all-time greats – hurdlers like Night Nurse or See You Then or Istabraq – could gain lengths at each flight. You don't get too many iffy jumpers winning the Champion.

QUEEN MOTHER CHAMPION CHASE

On a par with those two headline races, in terms of the appreciation from the racing public if not from the wider world, is the Queen Mother Champion Chase, run at breakneck pace over two miles of the Old Course on the second day of the meeting.

PREVIOUS SPREAD: Binocular at the last flight of the 2010 Smurfit Kappa Champion Hurdle. You can see why AP describes him as 'a proper hurdler'.

Master Minded and Ruby Walsh in full flight when winning the 2009 Seasons Holidays Queen Mother Champion Chase.

Again, speed and jumping ability are of the essence here. The Queen Mother Champion Chase is an exhilarating race in which to ride, and I was lucky enough to win it on the Paul Nicholls-trained grey Call Equiname in 1999. Call Equiname was a very fragile horse who was not able to race enough to find a lasting place in the affections of the jump racing crowd, but on his day he was brilliant, and that was certainly his day.

He had won the Victor Chandler Chase, run that year at Kempton Park, *en route* to the Queen Mother Champion Chase, where he started second favourite behind Edredon Bleu, ridden by Tony McCoy for Henrietta Knight.

Call Equiname was simply superb. When you ride a really good horse you feel like you've gone no gallop, while in the same race on a lesser horse you'd feel that you've been flat out, and the 1999 Queen Mother Champion Chase was a textbook example of that. All the way round Call Equiname seemed to find his task so effortless that it felt as if we were cantering, but he had to be held up for a late run, so after the second last I took a pull to prevent his getting to the front too soon – and taking a pull after the second last is not something you do too often in a championship race at the Cheltenham Festival. Edredon

The 2010 Seasons Holidays Queen Mother Champion Chase: Big Zeb (Barry Geraghty) hits the big time as he leads Forpadydeplasterer (AP McCoy) after the last.

Bleu and Direct Route were both superb two-mile chasers (Edredon Bleu would win the Queen Mother Champion Chase the following year), but the fact that they were the only dangers as we turned into the straight did not bother me, for I knew that Call Equiname had tremendous raw ability – and sure enough, once I had let him pop over the last just behind Edredon Bleu he put in an amazing surge to climb the hill and win by 1¼ lengths.

That was a typical renewal of the Queen Mother Champion Chase: fast and furious, building up to a thrilling finish. But there have been many close finishes, and what really seems to mark the race out, and to make it such a huge favourite with the Festival crowd, is the number of times this race provides a heart-stopping climax: Barnbrook Again beating Waterloo Boy in 1990, for example, or Edredon Bleu beating poor Direct Route, who never won the race, by a short head in 2000. Badsworth Boy won three times in the 1980s, and in recent years there have been several dual winners – great favourites like Barnbrook Again, Viking Flagship, Moscow Flyer and Master Minded, and horses who were not able to stage a repeat but sent the stands delirious when they won, like Remittance Man (then ridden by Jamie Osborne) in 1992 or One Man in 1998.

In brief, the cream of two-mile chasers taking each other on, jumping at breakneck speed and hammering down the hill before the race builds to its trademark roof-raising finish makes the Queen Mother Champion Chase one of the great sights of the Cheltenham Festival.

This show business thing is overrated: John McCririck winds down after recording the 'Cheltenham' song to promote the 2010 Festival.

THE OTHER BIG RACES

The Festival's other championship events include the **Triumph Hurdle** for four-year-olds over 2 miles 1 furlong of the New Course, traditionally the opening race on Gold Cup day.

In jump racing terms, four-year-olds are real youngsters, and the Triumph, which invariably has a large field and is run at a fast pace, is a very tough task for such inexperienced horses. You need a horse who can really stay, because – as I said above – the configuration of the New Course means that there are only two flights of hurdles in the last seven furlongs or so of the race. Cheltenham demands a horse with a will to win, as there's no hiding place for the faint-hearted.

It is a measure of the demands of the Triumph Hurdle that so few winners have gone on to land the Champion Hurdle itself. Katchit in 2008 was a recent example, but he was only the third horse to do the double since the race was revived at Cheltenham in 1965 after being run at the now defunct Hurst Park: the others were Persian War (who won the Triumph in 1967) and Kribensis (1988). Triple Champion Hurdle winner See You Then had finished runner-up in the 1984 Triumph, and dual Champion winner Monksfield had filled the same position in 1976.

Yet another Triumph for Nicky Henderson: Soldatino (Barry Geraghty) wins the 2010 JCB Triumph Hurdle from Barizan (Tom O'Brien).

The lesson is: a Triumph Hurdle contender has to be exceptionally tough and resolute, and for future Champion Hurdle clues, don't confine yourself to the winner.

The **Ladbrokes World Hurdle**, run over three miles of the New Course on the third day of the Festival, is the championship race for staying hurdlers, and as such is what we might call a niche race. For staying hurdlers form a division which is often dominated by a very select band of horses who might win this race more than once: horses like triple winner Inglis Drever or Big Buck's, who won in 2009 after a proposed chasing career had been abandoned and followed up in 2010. The way Big Buck's travelled through his races could be very deceptive – he often looked to be one of the first in trouble, yet he then would power away from his rivals, and at the line would still be putting more distance between him and the others – but however he gets to the winning post, he has been extraordinarily effective in getting there first!

Inglis Drever, who loved Cheltenham and always seemed to up his game there, with Denis O'Regan.

Obviously a horse needs stamina for the World Hurdle, but in spite of its distance the ability to jump hurdles at speed is still high on the list of qualities required: even in a three-mile hurdle, ground lost through sloppy jumping is hard to make up at the Festival.

A comparatively recent addition to the Festival menu has been the **Glenfarclas Cross-Country Chase** run over 3 miles 7 furlongs of the specially built course in the middle of the other courses. This features all manner of unorthodox obstacles – notably banks, based on the cross-country course at Punchestown – and presents a special challenge to any jockey: a challenge not just of horsemanship, but of navigation and the ability to memorise a route. I rode in the very first cross-country race at Cheltenham, and assiduously walked the course with a map in my hand, trying to drill into my brain all the twists and turns. I never managed to ride a winner over the course – I never took the wrong course

Connaught

The Glenfarclas Cross-Country Chase in full flow.

either! – but am convinced that some horses relish the novelty of it, and at the Festival it provides an opportunity for horses who would not normally be good enough to take part in one of the more orthodox races. Some dyed-in-the-wool racing purists are still sceptical about the race, but in my view its worth is illustrated by the hordes of people who leave the stands and go out into the middle to watch it. True jump racing enthusiasts like nothing better than to get really near to the action, to feel at close quarters the speed at which horses jump, and the cross-country allows them to have an experience far different from just going down to a fence or hurdle for a 'normal' race.

The two main novice hurdles at the Festival are the **Supreme Novices' Hurdle** over 2 miles 110 yards and run as the opening race of the week – accompanied by that wonderful spontaneous roar from the crowd which signals the proper beginning of a great week of racing and craic – and the **Neptune Investment**

OPPOSITE: Big Buck's and Ruby Walsh, an irresistible combination, winning the 2009 Ladbrokes World Hurdle.

holidays.com

Another great Cheltenham Festival favourite: Willie Wumpkins (Jim Wilson), three-time winner of the Coral Hurdle – 1979, 1980 and 1981.

PREVIOUS SPREAD: Theatre of dreams: the finish of the 2010 Weatherbys Champion Bumper, with Cue Card (Joe Tizzard) surging clear to win at 40-1.

Management Novices' Hurdle over 2 miles 5 furlongs on the second day, while the **Albert Bartlett Novices' Hurdle** over three miles attracts out-and-out stayers. The **Weatherbys Champion Bumper** is a National Hunt Flat race – that is, an obstacle-free race for future jumpers – over 2 miles 110 yards for four-, five- and six-year-olds, and over the years has given racegoers an early glimpse of future stars, such as Florida Pearl, who won in 1997. The bumper gives horses an opportunity to display their talents without the added pressure of jumping, and gives punters a chance to get stuck into an Irish hotpot, which they love to do!

Novice chasers are catered for in the **Irish Independent Arkle Challenge Trophy** over two miles, often won by a horse who will move on to run in the Queen Mother Champion Chase the following year, and the **RSA Chase** over 3 miles 110 yards is for staying novices with aspirations to the Gold Cup itself.

The quality of the **Ryanair Chase** over 2 miles 5 furlongs is advertised by the fact that 2009 winner Imperial Commander went on to win the 2010 Gold Cup.

Then there are the great handicaps which provide some of the most frenzied punting of the week, such as the **William Hill Trophy**, a chase over 3 miles 110 yards; the **Coral Cup Handicap Hurdle** over 2 miles 5 furlongs; the **Vincent O'Brien County Hurdle**, named to commemorate the great Irish trainer who, before reaching the pinnacle of arguably the best trainer ever on the Flat, won the Champion Hurdle three times and Gold Cup four times; and the **Johnny Henderson Grand Annual Chase** over 2 miles 110 yards, which commemorates Nicky Henderson's father, a long-time director at Cheltenham and one of the people who made the Festival what it is today.

The amateur tradition is a very important component of the magic of Cheltenham. Indeed, the birth of the Festival was when

the National Hunt Steeplechase, centrepiece of an annual gathering of racing and hunting people which began in 1859 and moved from place to place, settled at Cheltenham in 1911, and the **National Hunt Chase Challenge Cup** for amateur riders – popularly known as 'The Four-Miler' – is the longest race of the Festival, and one held in great affection by Cheltenham regulars. The amateurs also have the **Christie's Foxhunter Chase**, most prestigious hunter chase of the calendar and run over the Gold Cup course of 3 miles 2½ furlongs, and the **Fulke Walwyn Kim Muir Challenge Cup** over a furlong shorter.

Those are some of the highlights, but remember: all Cheltenham Festival races are big races to those who take part in them.

Stars of the future in the 2010 Neptune Investment Management Novices' Hurdle – and stars not only over jumps. Winner Peddlers Cross (Jason Maguire, right) went on to win at Aintree; runner-up Reve De Sivola (Daryl Jacob, centre) won at the big Punchestown meeting; and third-placed Rite Of Passage (Robbie McNamara, left) won the Gold Cup at Royal Ascot!

FOLLOWING SPREAD: Please don't let the favourite win! A bookmakers'-eye view of the Four-Miler in 2008.

JOE CHAD
RACING
Bob Stock

GRAHAM THORPE
GLYN JONES
R & J Racing

GREAT FESTIVAL MOMENTS

Given all the different elements which make the Festival the glorious occasion it is – the *craic*, the fierce Anglo-Irish rivalry, the history, the demands of the course itself – it's scarcely surprising that it has been the venue for a succession of unforgettable races which mark the great historic high points of jump racing. There are dozens which I could choose, but I'll confine myself to these, my Cheltenham Festival Six of the Best.

ARKLE and MILL HOUSE, 1964

For fevered anticipation, there has never been a race like it.

Arkle and Mill House were two outstanding young chasers. Both were seven years old, both were at the very top of their game, both looked unbeatable.

Mill House – 'The Big Horse', and winner of the Gold Cup the previous year – was Irish-bred and ridden by Irishman Willie Robinson, but trained in Lambourn by Fulke Walwyn. Arkle was Irish through and through: bred in County Dublin; ridden by Pat Taaffe (who had ridden Mill House in the horse's early years); trained near Dublin by Tom Dreaper; and owned by County Cork-born Anne, Duchess of Westminster.

They had already met once, in the 1963 Hennessy Gold Cup at Newbury, when Mill House had won easily, with Arkle only third. It transpired that Arkle had stumbled after putting his foot in a hole at the final open ditch and had been unable to recover fully, but for the Mill House camp that was just an excuse.

Make no mistake. This was a race which, much more fiercely than Kauto Star and Denman, divided the racing public into camps: Mill House was running for England, Arkle for Ireland.

The greatest: Arkle and Pat Taaffe clear of Mill House and Willie Robinson at the last fence in the 1964 Gold Cup.

Between Newbury and Cheltenham, both horses remained unbeaten. Mill House won the King George VI Chase at Kempton Park and the Gainsborough Chase at Sandown Park, while Arkle was unextended in three chases in Ireland.

The young giants scared off most of the Gold Cup opposition, and only two other horses lined up: Pas Seul, winner of the race in 1960 but now a shadow of his former self, and King's Nephew, a good handicap chaser but not in the same class as the young heroes. That this was a real two-horse race was confirmed by the starting prices: 8-13 Mill House, 7-4 Arkle, 20-1 bar two.

In those days the Gold Cup started from a chute beside the grandstand, and by the time the four runners came into view of the majority of the people packing the stands, Willie Robinson already had Mill House swinging along in the lead, with Pat Taaffe trying to restrain Arkle in his wake. As they came past the stands after a

'Himself' surveying his kingdom: the Arkle statue overlooking the old parade ring, before it was moved to its present position by Cheltenham's Arkle Bookshop.

circuit Mill House was still ahead, but every time he increased the pace, Arkle effortlessly went with him.

Mill House at full gallop was an awesome sight. At the top of the hill the outsiders had long since fallen away and he was still leading, but he could not shake off Arkle. At the second last Mill House still had a narrow lead, but it was clearly on sufferance. As the pair came round the final bend – this was the Old Course, with one fence to jump in the straight – Pat Taaffe did no more than shake the reins at Arkle, and the hope of all Ireland scooted clear and nipped over the last a couple of lengths to the good. Mill House seemed to rally after landing, but with Peter O'Sullevan declaring to BBC television viewers that 'This is the champion!', Arkle scurried up the hill to win by five lengths.

Arkle remained the champion until the untimely end of his racing career (see pages 194–8), and while Mill House took him on three more times, The Big Horse was never to lay another glove on his rival.

The 1964 Gold Cup was a race so famous that there were even poems and songs written about it in Ireland, telling how the Irish had put the English to the sword. And in racing terms there was simply nothing like it as far as build-up and excited anticipation were concerned. It was, as one writer was to put it, 'The day Arkle became a god.'

MONKSFIELD and SEA PIGEON, 1979

The 1970s is often described as the golden age of hurdling, and it's not hard to see why. This period saw a succession of iconic hurdling stars – who faced each other year after year and produced some of the most memorable horse races ever.

No jump racing fan will ever forget the likes of Persian War, Bula, Comedy Of Errors, Lanzarote and Night Nurse, but for a race which seemed to sum up that golden age I'd go for the amazing battle between Monksfield and Sea Pigeon in the 1979 Champion Hurdle.

Monksfield, trained in Ireland by Des McDonogh, was a diminutive horse and – unusually for a jumper – an entire, not a gelding. He had been narrowly beaten in the 1976 Triumph Hurdle at the Festival, and in 1977 had graduated to the Champion Hurdle, where he had run Night Nurse to two lengths, and then staged a famous dead-heat with the same horse in the Templegate Hurdle at Aintree. (See page 42.)

The little Irish horse reached the very top of the hurdling tree when, ridden by Mick Kinane's father Tommy, he came away from Night Nurse at the second last hurdle to win the 1978 Champion

Monksfield (Dessie Hughes, left) and Sea Pigeon (Jonjo O'Neill), who won four Champion Hurdles between them, inseparable at the last in 1979.

Hurdle, with Sea Pigeon, who had appeared to be cruising at the last, second.

Sea Pigeon had been a high-class horse on the Flat – good enough to run in the 1973 Derby, where he finished seventh behind Morston – but by now was combining handicaps on the level with the major hurdle races. He had won the Scottish Champion Hurdle in 1977, and after his Champion defeat in 1978 went to Ayr and won that race again.

The ante-post market for the Champion Hurdle had favoured Sea Pigeon over Monksfield, but as the rain fell on Cheltenham on the morning of the race his price drifted, so that it was Monksfield – ridden this time by Dessie Hughes, father of current top Flat jockey Richard – who went off favourite at 9-4, with Sea Pigeon 6-1. Among their rivals was Birds Nest, a tip-top hurdler who sometimes experienced steering problems and was now running in the race for the fourth time, Beacon Light, who had run in two previous Champion Hurdles, and young pretenders Connaught Ranger and Kybo. (When the latter's owner Isidore Kerman had been at boarding school, his mother had always signed off her letters to him with 'KYBO', for 'Keep Your Bowels Open'.)

By the time of the Champion Hurdle – run in those days on the middle day of the three-day meeting – the going was bottomless. This was going to be a slog.

At every flight Monksfield had the lead, but coming down to the second last plenty of the others were queuing up behind him. Then Kybo fell and the others started to fade, leaving Sea Pigeon the only threat to a Monksfield repeat.

Jonjo O'Neill had brought Sea Pigeon up the inside and they appeared to be cruising, while Dessie Hughes had already given Monksfield a smack. Look at that photo of them locked together at the last, Jonjo grinning in anticipation of a cheeky victory and Dessie having another crack in mid-air. Which looks the winner?

But appearances are deceptive. Monksfield, one of the gamest horses ever to look through a bridle, stuck his head down and his neck out and battled, battled, battled all the way up the hill. With fifty yards to go it still looked as if Sea Pigeon would win, but Monksfield knew better. A few strides from the post he forced his head in front, and got the verdict by three quarters of a length.

It had been a titanic battle, perhaps the greatest ever seen in the Champion Hurdle, and it is a measure of how well these two battle-hardened warriors took their races that a year later they came to the last flight in the Champion Hurdle together again, for the third year running. This time – when the race was run on better going on the first day of the Festival, and when the distance was a furlong shorter on account of a reconfiguration of the course – it was Sea Pigeon who prevailed. By the time he won for the second time in 1981, when ridden with unbelievable confidence by John Francome, Monksfield had retired to stud.

Next time someone tells you that hurdle racing is less enthralling a spectacle than chasing – there are such people around – show them a recording of Monksfield and Sea Pigeon in the 1979 Champion Hurdle. They might think differently then.

DAWN RUN, 1986

Given what I said about Dawn Run's Gold Cup at the head of this chapter, you won't be surprised to see it in my list of the very best Cheltenham occasions. It was a tumultuous race, a victory chiselled out of granite rather than the imperious sweep to the throne of Arkle in 1964.

Trained in Ireland by Paddy Mullins and owned by 'The Galloping Granny', Mrs Charmian Hill – who had ridden the mare herself in her first three bumpers, winning once – Dawn Run was not the best-looking horse ever to grace Cheltenham, but there was something quite irresistible about her attitude and her spirit. Jonjo O'Neill, who won both the Champion Hurdle and Gold Cup on her, once wrote: 'She was very moody, and for me at least not a very comfortable ride. I never felt that I really fitted into her neatly and tidily.'

By Gold Cup day 1986 Dawn Run had proved herself a very good hurdler, with many big-race wins including the Irish Champion Hurdle at Leopardstown, the 1984 Champion Hurdle, the Aintree Hurdle and two valuable hurdles at Auteuil. In the last three of those she was partnered by Paddy Mullins's son Tony, who had ridden her often in her early career.

Her first season over steeplechase fences had been badly curtailed by injury and she was only able to run once, winning at Navan. She added two more chasing wins in December 1985 before her still novicey jumping caught out Tony Mullins at the open ditch at the top of the Cheltenham hill in the big pre-Gold Cup chase at the end of January. He was unseated – and again lost the big-race ride in favour of Jonjo.

No horse had ever won both the Champion Hurdle and Gold Cup, though in recent memory a couple of the all-time hurdling greats had come close. Bula, winner of the Champion Hurdle in 1971 and 1972, had been third behind Ten Up in impossible going in 1975, and Night Nurse, Champion Hurdler in 1976 and 1977, had finished runner-up to Little Owl in 1981.

To be frank, Dawn Run was not in the same class as those two as a hurdler but, even though the Gold Cup would be only her fifth

Jonjo and Dawn Run early on.

ever race over fences, there was a widespread feeling that she had the brute strength to pull off the unique double, and she started 15-8 favourite.

This Gold Cup had echoes of the 1964 race, for Dawn Run was representing Ireland, and all the most fancied horses were trained in England. The first three in the 1985 Gold Cup – Forgive'N Forget, Righthand Man and Earl's Brig – were all back for more, and Wayward Lad, who the previous Christmas had won his third King George VI Chase, looked to have a real chance. Then there was Run And Skip, winner of the Welsh National, and Combs Ditch, fresh from a good win at Haydock. All in all, it was a typically strong Gold Cup field, and Dawn Run would do well to overcome her inexperience and win it.

Dawn Run's date with history looks unlikely at the last, where she's led by Wayward Lad (Graham Bradley) and Forgive'N Forget (Mark Dwyer, left).

Dawn Run did not take kindly to restraint, and Jonjo has memorably declared how 'we went to the first like shit off a shovel' – and for most of the first circuit and a half the mare vied for the lead with Run And Skip. Her jumping was far from perfect – she dropped her hind legs in the water second time round and clouted the fifth from home – but such was her iron constitution that these mistakes, which would have had a less robust horse hoisting the white flag, seemed to have little effect on her, and as the field turned down the hill she continued to dispute the lead with Run And Skip – though Wayward Lad and Forgive'N Forget, were getting closer.

At the third last – the final fence before the turn to face the hill and the last two jumps – she was just behind Run And Skip and under increasing pressure, but Dawn Run was never a horse to fold meekly, and she stuck to her guns. A spring-heeled leap at the second last brought her back into the lead, but Wayward Lad and Forgive'N Forget, passed her going to the last, and her cause looked lost. Then Forgive'N Forget, made a mistake at the last and handed the initiative to Wayward Lad, but he started wandering left as he reached the dregs of his stamina, and this gave Jonjo some hope. 'I suddenly saw he was tiring,' he said afterwards, 'and so did she' – and Dawn Run staged one final, remarkable rally. Fifty yards from the line it still looked as if Wayward Lad would hold on, but he was out on his feet and completely drained, while the rejuvenated Dawn Run was finding reserves of energy from God knows where.

I can still hear Peter O'Sullevan's famous commentary calling, 'The mare's gonna get up!' – and somehow Dawn Run clawed her way up those final few yards of the Cheltenham hill to catch Wayward Lad and win by a length.

After witnessing such a finish, it's no wonder that for me the idea of riding at Cheltenham became a beacon. It was something I just had to do.

The triumphant return.

If the race was tumultuous, that was as nothing to the scenes that followed. The hundreds of hats flung into the air as Dawn Run passed the post were just the prelude to pandemonium engulfing Cheltenham. Jonjo was submerged in a sea of embraces all the way to the winner's enclosure, where the mayhem continued unabated, with Mrs Hill being lifted onto the shoulders of Dawn Run fans.

This bedlam was simultaneously a recognition of a unique Cheltenham feat – and one, remember, that has not been repeated in the two and a half decades since then – and an outpouring of appreciation for a very Irish achievement.

No other Cheltenham winner in my time – not even Desert Orchid or Istabraq or Denman or Kauto Star – has triggered quite the reception that greeted Dawn Run after the 1986 Gold Cup.

With regard to what happened to the mare after the Gold Cup, read the account of her life on pages 201–3. For now, we should leave her swamped by her delirious fans. Cheltenham has never really seen anything like it, and I will never – ever – forget that sight. It changed my life.

DESERT ORCHID'S GOLD CUP, 1989

By Gold Cup day 1989, Desert Orchid was a national treasure. Inside racing and outside, everybody loved him, and no wonder. His colour, his attitude, his spring-heeled jumping, his indomitable courage – you name it, Dessie had it.

With one troubling exception. What he didn't have was his name on the Gold Cup roll of honour. He'd won a bucketful of big races, including the Whitbread in 1988 and the King George VI Chase in 1986 and 1988, and earlier in the 1988-89 season he had come out best after thrilling run-in battles with Panto Prince at Ascot and Pegwell Bay at Sandown Park.

But he hadn't won the Gold Cup, and if he were to have a proper claim to the greatness which everyone willed upon him, he had to do that.

To be honest, he didn't really seem to like Cheltenham, and he certainly didn't like bottomless going – so when the morning of Gold Cup day brought not only heavy rain but snow pouring over Cleeve Hill and onto the racecourse, it was as if the gods had turned against him. Deep puddles were forming on the track. The rain was coming in torrents, and so were the questions. Would racing take place? If it did, would Dessie run? And if he ran, could he possibly do himself justice?

The grey horse's connections, fronted by trainer David Elsworth and part-owner Richard Burridge, were not known for their faint-hearted attitude. They had run their hero over all sorts of distances

Desert Orchid (Simon Sherwood) in his customary front-running role before the race heats up. Note that Simon, unlike the other jockeys, is not wearing goggles: there was no need when riding Dessie!

and in all sort of conditions, and they were not going shirk his greatest challenge now. With the proviso that jockey Simon Sherwood would pull him up if he was clearly hating the ground, Dessie would run.

His twelve opponents included the two most recent winners, The Thinker (1987) and Charter Party (1988); Bonanza Boy, who had won the Welsh National; Carvill's Hill, the great hope of Ireland but a horse running in only his fifth chase and a dodgy jumper; Ten Plus, winner of his last four races and trained by the legendary Fulke Walwyn, who had won the race four times; West Tip, winner of the 1986 Grand National; and, among the outsiders, the mud-loving Yahoo.

Desert Orchid was available at 7-2 in the betting ring before a surge of sentimental money brought him in to 5-2: an uneasy favourite, but those bookies who decided to take him on would soon learn the lesson that sometimes in racing – just sometimes – sentiment does prevail.

Dessie made the early running in his usual fashion, closely attended by his rivals. Golden Freeze, Carvill's Hill and The Thinker fell on the first circuit, but the grey, while clearly not enjoying the conditions and not able to jump with his usual verve, kept the lead, and going out into the country for the second circuit the dream was still alive.

Ten Plus took up the running ('It gave my horse a bit of a rest,' said Simon Sherwood later), and by the turn downhill the race had moved into top gear. Desert Orchid hit the fourth last hard and Ten Plus pressed on with even greater power – then slammed into the third last, fell and broke a pastern, a tragic footnote to a sensational race.

That left only Desert Orchid and Yahoo slugging it out over the final quarter mile, and coming to the second last it was Yahoo going the better. He landed a length to the good, but the collective will pouring down from the stands seemed to lift Desert Orchid back into contention. The two were wide apart as they came to the last

Just after the last fence, Yahoo and Tom Morgan still have the lead, but Dessie is about to get up.

and Yahoo still had a narrow lead – and on the run-in the outsider, who had the advantage of the far rail, went further ahead as Desert Orchid, dead tired, started to wander towards the stands side. Simon wrenched him back onto an even keel and started to close the gap, but it was now as if the race was being run in slow motion. Desert Orchid veered towards Yahoo, Simon straightened him again, and then somehow, with the winning post looming, Dessie got his head in front and kept it there to win by a length and a half.

It had not been fluent and it had not been pretty, but it had put Desert Orchid's reputation beyond argument.

Job done.

EDREDON BLEU and DIRECT ROUTE, 2000

The Queen Mother Champion Chase is tailor-made to produce memorable finishes, but few have been as stirring as the 2000 race when Edredon Bleu and Direct Route produced one of the most exciting climaxes that Festival veterans can remember.

One of the great joys of the Queen Mother Champion Chase is its continuity. Year after year, the principals include horses who have run prominently in the race before, and the 2000 renewal was strong in that regard. I had won the 1999 race on Call Equiname from Edredon Bleu, a wonderfully exuberant and consistent chaser trained by Henrietta Knight, with Direct Route, trained by Howard Johnson, third – and although Call Equiname had had all sorts of problems in the 1999-2000 season and could not try for the double, both Edredon Bleu and Direct Route were back for another crack at the two-mile crown.

Neither started favourite, that position going to Flagship Uberalles on the strength of his having won the Haldon Gold Cup at Exeter, the Tingle Creek Chase at Sandown – beating both Edredon Bleu and Direct Route at level weights – and the Game Spirit Chase at Newbury, and finishing a gallant second to

Nordance Prince in the Victor Chandler Handicap Chase at Ascot.

Edredon Bleu had won the Peterborough Chase at Huntingdon for the second time in November 1999 but had then run third in the Tingle Creek and again third in a Sandown handicap, while Direct Route had been narrowly beaten in both the Haldon Gold Cup and Tingle Creek Chase and then finished fourth behind

All to play for at the last: left to right, Edredon Bleu (AP McCoy), Direct Route (Norman Williamson) and Flagship Uberalles (Joe Tizzard).

9

6

Nordance Prince, Flagship Uberalles and Celibate in the Victor Chandler Chase. Nordance Prince and Celibate were both in the Queen Mother Champion Chase line-up – the latter ridden by me – but neither was strongly fancied to beat the three market leaders at level weights. At the off, Flagship Uberalles was a warm favourite at 11-10, with Edredon Bleu 7-2 and Direct Route 5-1.

I'd won the Arkle Chase over the same distance on Tiutchev the previous day in course record time, but the pace in the Queen Mother Champion Chase felt even stronger, and as Tony McCoy on the front-running Edredon Bleu started to turn up the heat at the fourth-last fence, Celibate struggled to go the pace.

Up ahead of us, though, the race was boiling into a fantastic showdown. After the fourth last, AP set Edredon Bleu alight and powered down the hill with Flagship Uberalles and Direct Route in hot pursuit – then Flagship hit the second last, handing the advantage to the other two. Flagship rallied, and at the last fence was upsides Direct Route and only marginally behind Edredon Bleu – but he started to fade as Edredon Bleu and Direct Route locked horns.

Eyeball to eyeball they climbed the hill, and halfway up the run-in Direct Route started to edge ahead – but then, under an inspired ride from AP McCoy, Edredon Bleu started to fight back. This was a real hammer-and-tongs finish if ever there was one, and with both horses and both jockeys giving their absolute all the stands went wild. In the shadow of the post, with Direct Route still clinging on to his tiny advantage, AP forced Edredon Bleu's nose in front, and they won by a short head, breaking Tiutchev's one-day-old course record in the process. Flagship Uberalles was six lengths back in third.

Edredon Bleu enjoyed other great days – he won the King George VI Chase at 25-1 in 2003 – and Direct Route was never to win at the Cheltenham Festival, but the finish they delivered in

OPPOSITE: Battle is joined in two unforgettable runnings of the Queen Mother Champion Chase. ABOVE, Waterloo Boy (Richard Dunwoody, near side) and winner Barnbrook Again (Hywel Davies) locked together at the last in 1990. BELOW, runner-up Travado (Jamie Osborne), third-placed Deep Sensation (Declan Murphy) and winner Viking Flagship (Adrian Maguire) at the same stage in 1994.

2000 will for ever remain one of the great Cheltenham Festival moments.

KAUTO STAR and DENMAN, 2008-2010

Not one great Festival race but three, and a rivalry which has lit up jump racing over the last few years.

The bare facts are simple enough.

Kauto Star and Denman were both foaled in 2000, both trained by Paul Nicholls, and have both won the Gold Cup.

2008: Sam Thomas and Denman go clear of Ruby Walsh and Kauto Star, who just hold off me and Neptune Collonges for second.

But the horses themselves are very different. Kauto Star is a French-bred bay with a large white blaze, Denman an Irish-bred chestnut with a white star. Kauto Star has tended to settle his races with a conclusive turn of foot, while Denman, living up to his nickname 'The Tank', wins his races by a display of relentless power. In short, Kauto Star is the modern sort of chaser: French-bred, versatile, full of speed. Denman is the old-fashioned Irish type: a big, long-striding galloper who slogs his rivals into submission.

2009: Revenge for Kauto Star, who romps home alone to regain the crown.

By the time of their first meeting, in the 2008 Totesport Cheltenham Gold Cup, they were both at the very top of the chasing tree.

Kauto Star was the reigning champion, having won the 2007 Gold Cup in brilliant style to crown a season in which he was unbeaten in six races, including the Tingle Creek Chase at Sandown Park and the King George VI Chase at Kempton – which underlines Kauto Star's versatility, as not many staying chasers would be as effective over the two miles of the Tingle Creek as they

would be over the three miles of the King George. (I'd ridden him when he won the Tingle Creek for the first time in 2005, and just loved the way he travelled so effortlessly through the race.)

Kauto Star's first race of the 2007-08 campaign saw him beaten at Aintree by Monet's Garden, and a month later in November 2007 Denman, his next-door neighbour in Paul Nicholls' yard, put in a handicap performance of near-Arkle proportions to win the Hennessy under top weight. All of a sudden jump racing had a potential rivalry to match that of 'Himself' and Mill House.

2010: Kauto Star has departed as AP McCoy drives Denman in vain pursuit of Imperial Commander and Paddy Brennan.

Denman's road to the top had been very different from that of his stable companion, who had won several races in France before being sold to owner Clive Smith. After winning a point-to-point in Ireland when trained by my former weighing-room colleague Adrian Maguire, Denman had been bought by Somerset dairy farmer Paul Barber – in whose colours I had won the Gold

Cup on See More Business – and a half share was sold on to the flamboyant gambler Harry Findlay. (The horse has run in Paul Barber's or Harry Findlay's colours in alternate years – though Harry gave up his share in the summer of 2010 in return for complete ownership of Grand National fourth Big Fella Thanks.)

Denman was a high-class novice hurdler, and when switched

Not much doubt which horse he's rooting for!

to fences went through the 2006–07 season unbeaten, culminating in a demolition of his rivals in the Royal & SunAlliance Chase at the 2007 Festival. He was clearly a very good chaser indeed, but that 2007 Hennessy was something else. Ridden by Sam Thomas as Ruby Walsh was injured, he beat Dream Alliance eleven lengths with an astounding display of powerful galloping and a series of tremendous jumps.

After that, jump racing fans could hardly wait to see him take on Kauto Star in the 2008 Gold Cup, and the ante-post market suggested a close race. After Newbury, Denman went to Leopardstown to win the Lexus Chase, then back to Newbury for an easy prep in the Aon Chase – so he was going into the Gold Cup unbeaten in steeplechases.

Meanwhile, Kauto Star had won the Betfair Chase at Haydock (again ridden by Sam, as Ruby was still injured), and had taken a second King George before completing his pre-Cheltenham race programme with a facile victory in the Ascot Chase.

The build-up to the first meeting of these great chasers carried echoes of the weeks approaching the famous 1964 Gold Cup showdown between Arkle and Mill House, and debate had been raging for months about the outcome. Early in Festival week one leading bookmaker was going 11-10 each of two, but by the day of the race there seemed to be significantly more confidence around Kauto Star than around Denman, and Kauto started odds-on favourite at 10-11, with Denman comparatively easy to back at 9-4.

I had been booked to ride the third Paul Nicholls runner Neptune Collonges, and we led for the first circuit before Sam Thomas moved Denman alongside at the fence in front of the stands and set off into the country. From where I was sitting I could tell that 'The Tank' at full throttle would take some catching, and with Kauto Star jumping less fluently than usual, the writing was very much on the wall.

At the fourth last Ruby went for his whip on Kauto Star, but Denman was powering along like a force of nature. He turned into the straight with a long lead, hammered over the last two fences and, although getting tired, kept on up the hill to beat Kauto Star seven lengths – and Neptune Collonges almost got up for second, finishing just a short head behind Kauto, making a remarkable one-two-three for Paul Nicholls.

It had been an exhilarating display by Denman, but his time in the sun was short. In September 2008 it was reported that he was working disappointingly, and he was diagnosed with an irregular heartbeat. After treatment he was sidelined, not reappearing on a racecourse until February 2009, only five weeks before the Festival – and his Kempton Park return was a desperate anti-climax, as he traipsed home a very tired horse 23 lengths behind that season's Hennessy winner Madison Du Berlais.

After his defeat by Denman in the 2008 Gold Cup, Kauto Star seemed to lose his way for a while, narrowly beaten by Our Vic at Aintree in his last race of the 2007-08 season and unseating Sam Thomas at the last fence at Haydock, scoring a bloodless success at Down Royal in between. But then he won a third King George in brilliant style, and the chance of his becoming the only horse ever to regain the Gold Cup crown after losing it looked very much on the cards.

Kauto Star started 7-4 favourite for the 2009 Gold Cup and put up a sensational display to win by 13 lengths from Denman, who had started 8-1 second favourite and, significantly, had run a much more restrained race than in the all-guns-blazing victory the previous year. He had not won but he was well and truly rehabilitated, and the Cheltenham crowd gave him a hugely affectionate reception when he came into the unsaddling enclosure. To experience a jump race crowd at its best, be in the Festival stands as an honourably beaten horse is greeted.

FOLLOWING SPREAD: Friends as well as rivals – Denman and Kauto Star on their summer holiday at Paul Nicholls's yard.

Cottage Rake (Aubrey Brabazon up), winner of the Gold Cup in 1948, 1949 and 1950.

Denman went on to Aintree, where he took a crashing fall at the second last when looking likely to be involved in the finish – and then it was time to join Kauto Star for their summer break.

In mid November, Kauto Star was at Haydock for his first race of the season and after a titanic struggle with Imperial Commander got home by a nose – which had recently been introduced into the official form book as a narrower margin than 'short head' – and a week later Denman returned to Newbury for another Hennessy. With Ruby Walsh in the saddle, he won the race for a second time with a power-packed display which proclaimed the return of the Denman of old.

Then Kauto Star proved himself as magnificent as ever by beating Madison Du Berlais 36 lengths to win his fourth King George in a row, a feat not accomplished before.

The old rivalry was back, and the racing authorities started cranking up the excitement which would erupt on Gold Cup day at Cheltenham. It was a marketing man's dream – there were scarves in the respective owners' colours, rosettes, lapel buttons and all sorts of other favours proclaiming loyalty to one horse or the other (though I did hear that there was an old codger at Kempton on King George day who insisted on wearing a scarf in the Arkle colours!).

After the King George it was confirmed that Kauto Star would go straight to Cheltenham, while Denman would return to Newbury in February for his Gold Cup warm-up in the Aon Chase. Ridden by Tony McCoy, who would ride him in the Gold Cup as stable jockey Ruby Walsh had stayed loyal to Kauto Star, Denman blotted his copybook again, blundering badly at the fourth last and a fence later unshipping AP.

A far from ideal Cheltenham prep, and the wind had gone out of the sails of the big showdown, for Kauto Star was looking by far the likelier winner, while Denman had it all to prove yet again.

As the tapes rose on the 2010 Gold Cup, Kauto Star was a warm 8-11 favourite, with Denman 4-1 and Imperial Commander – trained by Nigel Twiston-Davies, ridden by Paddy Brennan, and a real Cheltenham specialist – third favourite on 7-1, despite having finished way behind Kauto Star in the King George earlier in the season.

Less restrained than in 2009, Denman shared the early running with Carruthers – bred and co-owned by the ever-popular John Oaksey – before taking over with a circuit to race, but after an almighty mistake at the eighth fence Kauto Star was never travelling easily, and was struggling when he got the fourth last all wrong and took a crunching fall. Denman was still leading at the turn into the straight, but Imperial Commander took over at the second last and stayed on stoutly up the hill to win by seven lengths.

Denman had turned in another heroic Gold Cup performance and received another huge welcome back, but his season was not finished. He went over to Punchestown for the Guinness Gold Cup and gave a textbook display of how some horses are affected by the direction of the course. All Denman's best runs have been on left-handed courses – notably Cheltenham and Newbury – and he clearly hated the right-hand turns of Punchestown, being hard pressed to finish fourth behind Planet Of Sound. 'Nothing ventured, nothing gained,' said Paul Nicholls afterwards, but you could bet your bottom dollar that Denman would not race right-handed again.

Whether the rivalry between Denman and Kauto Star has another chapter or not remains to be seen, but one thing is for certain: this pair of outstanding horses have given us some wonderful Cheltenham Festival memories.

And memories are what the Cheltenham Festival delivers year after year, in a manner unlike anything else in sport. You can see why I think it's a magical occasion.

Another triple Gold Cup hero: Best Mate and Jim Culloty winning their first Tote Cheltenham Gold Cup in 2002.

RACECOURSES

11

PREVIOUS SPREAD: Ludlow – where I rode my first winner.

It may be a cliché that the variety of British and Irish racecourses is one of the major factors in jump racing's popularity, but that doesn't stop it being true. From the great stages like Cheltenham or Aintree to the more homely charms of Sedgefield or Fakenham, each course is different in configuration and – even more important as far as the appeal of the sport is concerned – in character.

Racegoers absolutely love that variety, and so do the jockeys, because each different course has its own nuances and idiosyncrasies, and so each poses a different set of problems to a rider – and the more you ride on a particular track, the more you get to know how to ride it.

During my riding career I rode on every jumps track in Britain and all in Ireland bar Downpatrick and Kilbeggan – though Ffos Las in south Wales, Britain's newest racecourse and already very popular with the jump jockeys as well as the Flat, opened too late for me. And Wolverhampton, Windsor and Nottingham are courses where I rode winners but no longer stage jump racing.

I don't claim to have a 'favourite' course, and certainly don't have a least favourite, though I have to say that Market Rasen always seemed such a difficult course to get to from my home near Lambourn: there seemed to be no short cuts, and no matter how hard or fast I drove, it always took an age to reach. Mind you, the return journey from any course, however far flung, was much quicker if I'd had a winner or two …

It has always intrigued me that many jumping tracks have a very different aspect from the jockey's point of view, compared with how the riders in the stands see them.

Take **Kempton Park**, which by any measure is one of my favourite racecourses. Nicky Henderson, the trainer with whom I was

most closely associated in my career, loved the place and always targeted it for specific types of horse, and I rode plenty of winners there. Indeed, my first winner as Nicky's stable jockey was at Kempton, on Billy Bathgate in a novice chase in October 1993.

Plenty of so-called experts will tell you that Kempton is a sharp, easy track which suits the nimble sort of horse more than the long-striding galloper, and therefore Kempton form is to be treated very warily when assessing the chances of a horse at the much more wide open and undulating courses at Cheltenham. Nothing could be further from the truth: indeed, I would go so far as to say that Kempton is the closest you could get to a trial track for Cheltenham. Yes, one is flat and the other up hill and down dale; and yes, one is right-handed and the other left-handed; but the characteristics you need in a Kempton winner are exactly the same as those you look

'Out in the country' – if you can call it that – at Kempton Park.

for in a potential Cheltenham winner. At both courses, if you are not travelling – 'travelling' is how jockeys describe a horse going well within himself until things start to boil up in earnest – you won't get home. And if you don't get home, don't jump well and accurately at speed, and don't fully stay, you won't win at either course.

Admittedly a horse that wins Kempton's biggest prize, the King George VI Chase on Boxing Day, will not always go on to perform as well in the Gold Cup at Cheltenham, and vice versa, but the key difference between those two great races is the most obvious one: the distance of the King George is three miles, while the distance of the Gold up is three and a quarter miles, and that quarter mile can make all the difference.

Desert Orchid drew the crowds to Kempton in their thousands. Here he's winning the 1990 King George VI Rank Chase under Richard Dunwoody, Dessie's fourth win in the race.

One of the reasons why Kempton was such a favourite of mine is that while it looks such a straightforward a place to ride, it's not.

When a jockey comes back into the changing room after riding a good horse in an ordinary race, you'll often hear him say how slow they went, while a jockey who rode a lesser horse who was always struggling to hold his position in the same race will think they went flat out. What lies behind such different perceptions is simply the cruising speed of their respective horses.

As a jockey becomes more experienced, the races in which he rides seem to become slower, much as a top-class seasoned footballer seems to create space around him. When I started riding it felt like every race was over in a flash, and I could hardly wait for the next chance, whereas the older and wiser you get, the further ahead you seem to be able to think. And when you're experienced you seem to be able to see the next hurdle or fence even as you're jumping the one before it – a bit like a snooker player who is thinking not just about the ball he is playing, but the ball after that, and further ahead.

In race-riding, as in snooker, you're always plotting ahead. For instance, three quarters of the way through a race you'll be thinking about the horses around you: this one next to me is not travelling, and there's a chance that he'll make a mistake at this next fence as it's a tricky one, so I'd better move out from behind him. Or: he's jumping to the right at every fence, so I'll stay where I am, because if he jumps to the right again at the next he'll hamper one or two of the others around me, and I'll be in trouble. The more experienced you become, the more all those thought processes seem to happen in slow motion, and so the better you're able to pick up on them.

It's all very well trying to make up ground, but Kempton is a very difficult course on which to ride the perfect waiting race. If you give your horse a breather coming round the home turn, by the time you're into the straight the leaders might have gone, and you'll

JUMPS RACECOURSES IN BRITAIN AND IRELAND

be having to chase them. That's why over those last three fences you want to keep a little bit up your sleeve. If you save a little bit, you might have enough to get home.

At Kempton, where you're never far away from the next turn, the ability to save ground is essential, particularly on that long sweeping bend into the home straight. Unless I was riding an avowed front-running pillar-to-post type of horse, I used to like to get a lead into the straight so that I'd be saving a bit round the bend, and then start to make up my ground once we'd levelled out. Trying to make up ground round the bend risked giving away too much distance.

Down the back at Taunton.

In a chase at Kempton the positioning of the fences is something you have to think about. The fourth from home – that is, the last fence down the back straight – is a crucial stage of a steeplechase there, because it's followed by the long home turn and then three fences close together in the straight. Unlike on some tracks, where the final fences are more spaced out, at Kempton you need to know exactly what you're doing by the fourth last, and you need to be on the heels of the leaders.

I always used to try to fill a horse up – that is, get plenty of air into his lungs – as soon as we'd jumped the fourth last at Kempton, sitting up a bit in the saddle and tapping on the brake all the way round the bend, only asking for his final effort once we'd properly straightened up for home and were heading for the third last. The aim was to get the horse to relax for as long as possible before winding him up. Many horses tense up and breathe irregularly as soon as their jockey grabs hold of them with the reins, so the longer you can get them filling the lungs, the better. But if you're not travelling well at that stage you don't have the luxury of being able to take that little breather, which is why positioning throughout a race is so important.

The third last – that is, the first in the straight – is an absolutely crucial fence here, and it is no coincidence that a disproportionate number of horses fall or make race-losing mistakes there. A notable victim of this fence was Desert Orchid, who fell there in the last race of his career, the King George VI Chase in December 1991. He had won the King George four times and as a powerful front-runner was in his element at Kempton, but that third last caught him out and, like plenty of lesser horses before him, he paid the price. (It is curious to note that both Desert Orchid's first race – a novice hurdle in 1983 – and last race ended in falls at Kempton!)

The prime reason for the awkwardness of that fence, which in itself is quite small and inoffensive, is that it comes at a point when the race is on in earnest and horses are at full stretch and getting tired, and therefore more likely to make mistakes. Understandably, a tired horse is much more likely than a fresh one to put down at a fence when you've asked him to come up for you, and that third last at Kempton does catch them out.

A good jump at the third last will give you the momentum to take the second last in your stride, but the last has no margin for error. Make a mistake there and you have precious little time to put things right before the winning post – unlike, say, at Cheltenham, where the run-in is much longer and a stiff uphill climb, whereas Kempton's is short and flat.

On the face of it, **Ascot** is similar to Kempton, in that they're both right-handed triangles with a circuit of about a mile and three quarters. But Ascot is much more undulating, and any course with ups and downs presents problems for horses going into the fences – and, to a lesser extent, the hurdles.

Although there are particularly tricky fences like the downhill open ditch, from the jockey's point of view Ascot is a beautiful track to ride: a lovely wide course, with long sweeping bends. And it's an especially invigorating experience if you're on a genuine

front-runner who can jump accurately, as you can make up such a lot of ground at the fences.

Big screens – like this one at Ascot – add greatly to the racegoing experience.

If you're on a really top-class chaser, Ascot is a complete dream to ride. In November 1994 I rode Andrew and Madeleine Lloyd Webber's Raymylette there in the First National Bank Chase, and we had a memorable round.

Raymylette was already my favourite horse, and I'd been thrilled to ride him to win the Cathcart Challenge Cup at that year's Cheltenham Festival. Despite having form of that quality, he started at 10-1 for the Ascot race, perhaps because he was carrying top weight of 11st 10lb in what appeared a very competitive handicap over two and a half miles. I jumped him out of the gate and let him get into his own stride. He met every single fence perfectly, and then plugged on like the ultra-honest horse he was when Graham Bradley and Couldnt Be Better – a very good chaser who in a couple of weeks' time would win the

Hennessy Gold Cup at Newbury – came at us on the run-in. We won by a length.

The following month Raymylette and I were back at Ascot for the three-mile Betterware Cup (which started life back in the 1960s as the SGB Chase, and in 1966 was the last race won by Arkle).

Again I rode him from the front, letting him stride on and enjoy a good look at every fence, and again he jumped like a gazelle. At the last we were taken on by the mare Dubacilla, but again Raymylette rallied to regain the lead, and stayed on to win. Brilliant!

Pretty well upsides Cheltenham, Kempton Park and Ascot in my affections must be **Sandown Park** – one of the most popular jumping circuits in the country, especially over fences, and a very different riding proposition from the others.

In simple terms, the hurdles course sits alongside the Flat track and, with two flights of hurdles up the long straight, is pretty straightforward to ride. But from the home turn the chasing circuit takes a wholly different course from the hurdles track, and finishes at a different angle across the course, which can be very deceptive for spectators. (See the photo on pages 124-5.)

The best way to describe the thrill of riding round Sandown would be to hark back to the day in February 1995, when I rode Cuddy Dale, trained by Nicky Henderson for Her Majesty Queen Elizabeth the Queen Mother (who had been given the horse by his previous owner Geoff Hubbard), in a three-mile chase. The race was called the Stag Handicap Chase, and the way Cuddy Dale performed that day made me think that he must have read the racecard, for he jumped like a stag throughout.

A three-mile chase at Sandown starts at the top of the hill beyond the winning post. My intention had been to set off handy

Up the hill at Sandown Park.

rather than make the running, but as soon as the race started Cuddy Dale just grabbed the bit and was gone. The first fence, on the downhill run away from the stands, can be tricky at the best of times, and I'd intended just to let Cuddy Dale pop over it. But he took off from outside the wings of the fence and sailed over it as if it had been a hurdle, which took me by surprise, and then he set off round the turn to face that exhilarating run of seven fences down the Sandown back straight: three plain fences, then the water, and then the three notorious Railway Fences.

Ping! Ping! Ping! Cuddy Dale was breathtaking over the first three, then took the water in his stride and made for the Railway Fences. What makes this sequence of three plain fences such an important phase of any chase round Sandown is that they are very close together, and that on the final circuit they come at a crucial stage of the race, as things are really starting to heat up.

Whether on the first circuit or second time round, I always felt that the key to the Railway Fences was to pop over the first and then let your horse run into the second, and the instant you land over that one you squeeze him along to the third. It should take nine strides to

BETFRED.com
BETFRED.com RACING POST
BETFRED.com
skybet 08000 722 421
TRIPLEPRINT
DOUBLEPRINT
BETFRED.com

BETFRED.com
BETFRED.com
BETFRED.com
BETFRED.com
BETFRED.com
BETFRED.com

PREVIOUS SPREAD: The Sandown straight, illustrating graphically the different routes of the hurdles and chase courses.

get from the middle fence to the third, and it's vital to land running over the middle one if you want to meet the third spot on.

Again Cuddy Dale was sensational, meeting the first two exactly right and then taking off outside the wings at the third.

Then it was into that long, sweeping bend which takes you to the Pond Fence. There's a little incline into that fence, and the obstacle itself is not large, which would account for why there seem to be so few fallers there. That slope is a chance to get a breather into a horse, and since Cuddy Dale had been running with the choke out from the start, I thought it important to get him to relax. Then into the straight to take two fences: a plain fence and, on the first circuit, the open ditch in front of the stands. Many horses give that ditch a great deal of air – there's a famous photo of Arkle giving it about two feet in the 1965 Whitbread Gold Cup – and, as with the Pond Fence, you rarely seem to see a faller there. It's a nice fence, on a steady uphill – you can't apprcciate just how uphill the Sandown straight is unless you stand at its lowest point – and once a field of three-mile chasers is over that they tend to bunch up as the leaders take a breather before swinging right at the top of the hill and going out on the second circuit.

From the top of that hill it's a roller-coaster ride towards the fence on the downhill slope, and horses who are beginning to tire tend to make mistakes here as they get on their forehand and are liable to trip over themselves. At this stage of a staying chase at Sandown some of the lads on the slower runners think that downhill stretch is a chance to make some ground, and if you're among the leaders you can sense yourself being pushed along by the ones behind you.

But Cuddy Dale went hammering down to that fence as if someone had thrust a burning torch up his arse, and he flew over it – so quickly that we were immediately into the right-hand bend and again facing those seven fences down the back. He was as stag-like on the second circuit as he had been on the first, taking the Railway Fences and the Pond Fence just right and keeping his lead as we straightened up for the run for home, which on the second circuit has two plain fences.

The best way to ride Sandown from the Pond Fence is to save ground by hugging the rail round the bend and then squeeze down to the second last, forcing the guys coming to challenge you to come up the outside and thus give away ground. If you get on that inside rail and then scoot for home, you've stolen a bit of a margin, and with the last fence and the lung-breaking final climb to come, that can make all the difference.

Cuddy Dale did everything in textbook fashion and won by five lengths from Flyer's Nap.

When I came back in I said to Nicky: 'That's what chasing is all about.'

I never had a better ride round Sandown, and very few better ones anywhere else. It was just magic. But Sandown Park is that sort of place. It brings out the best in horses.

Along the far straight at Towcester.

Like Cheltenham, Sandown, Kempton and Ascot, **Aintree** attracts the cream of chasers and hurdlers, especially at the Grand National Festival meeting in April, which is now second only to the Cheltenham Festival as far as quality in depth is concerned.

I'll deal with the Grand National course itself in the section on that race (pages 156–91) and here confine myself to the smaller circuit, formally known as the Mildmay Course (after Lord Mildmay, who in the middle decades of the twentieth century was a hugely popular amateur rider – and whose great service to jump racing was that he introduced the Queen Mother to the sport).

Aintree has puzzled me more than any other track, and as often as not I'd walk away from there after a day's racing scratching my

Aintree: the open ditch in the straight, with the magnificent new stands in the background.

head and thinking: What is the right way to ride this place? And I wasn't the only jockey to find it strange.

It's another of those courses which belies its reputation. The circuit has two long straights and a tight configuration, which seems to have given everybody the idea that it's a very fast track. But look at the figures. The Raceform Median Time for a two-mile chase at Aintree – that is, the point at which half the recorded times for that course and distance over the last five years are slower, and half are faster – is 4 minutes 1.0 seconds, whereas the median time for a two-mile chase on the Old Course at Cheltenham is 3 minutes 59.3 seconds, and a two-mile chase at Kempton 3 minutes 54.8 seconds. That is hard evidence that Aintree is not nearly the tearaway fast track that everyone seems to take it to be.

But whatever the clock says, it's a very hard course to ride. If you say to yourself, 'Right – I'm going to drop my horse in behind the leaders and race well within my compass and then pick them off one by one,' you simply won't get there. By the time your horse has made his way through all the traffic he'll have emptied, and have nothing left for a final effort. You simply can't afford to be too far back, and you have to try to save ground on the bends.

I eventually came to the conclusion that the perfect way to ride Aintree would be to stay in fifth or sixth place until the heat is turned up coming out of the back straight, and I knew that in a chase it could be very hard to make up ground if the horses in front of you are going well.

But a part of me is still baffled.

Newbury, home of the Hennessy Cognac Gold Cup and Totesport Trophy, is a wonderful course from a jockey's point of view: a lovely spacious circuit of 1 mile 7 furlongs; wide and mostly flat; beautifully constructed fences (is it just Old Jockey Syndrome that makes me think they're getting easier?); and two long straights which demand you get your horse into a nice rhythm. At Newbury, rhythm is all.

Take a steeplechase over 3¼ miles, the distance of the Hennessy. You start at a chute off the beginning of the back straight, then take five fences down the back (plain fence, open ditch, three plain fences) before swinging left to face the cross fence, then an easy turn into the straight to take a plain fence, the second open ditch and two more plain fences before sweeping over the water jump. (Water jumps have been source of some controversy over the years, as too many horses were getting injured at them, even with the new structure of a very shallow level of water and minimal lip. Several courses have got rid of their water jumps, but I have no problem with them, so long as you treat them with due respect, as you would any other fence. Newbury is the prime example of the water jump providing a wonderful spectacle,

Heart-in-the-mouth stuff, but an awkward negotiation of the final hurdle won't stop Get Me Out Of Here and AP McCoy winning the 2010 Totesport Trophy.

and the nature of a chase there would be considerably altered – for the worse – if it were ever to be removed.)

Going out onto the second circuit at Newbury, it's even more crucial to keep in that rhythm and meet each fence on a roll, as horses are starting to get tired and more prone to making mistakes. Five fences down the back again, and second time round the cross fence is one of the most critical points of a Newbury chase, a place where a race can be won or lost. Get it right and you're swinging into the straight with that rhythm intact; get it wrong, and all of a sudden you're struggling.

Turning in at Newbury you're still well over half a mile from home, and on a tired horse you'll be counting every yard. In a chase, the third last is the final open ditch, another place where the tiny margin between getting it right and getting it wrong can make the difference between victory and defeat.

Newbury has a final trick up its sleeve after the last fence, as the water jump directly in front of the grandstand is cordoned off and you need to come round a right-handed elbow shortly before the winning post. This makes the position in which you jump the last fence a matter of huge importance. Too close to the inside rail and you'll have to yank hard right to get to the elbow, and unbalance your horse; too close to the stands side and you'll be leaving yourself open to someone nipping between you and the elbow and getting the rail for those crucial last few yards. So the knack is to take the last in the middle – but of course you won't be the only jockey to have thought of that, and when two or three are in contention it can get a bit crowded.

I always loved riding round Newbury, and won plenty of good races there: the 2005 Hennessy on Trabolgan (see pages 22–3) and three wins in the Tote Gold Trophy were the highlights, but I also have a special memory from Hennessy day in November 1997, Sir Peter O'Sullevan's very last afternoon commentating for BBC television. Sir Peter was always a great friend to the jockeys: he had a profound understanding of all aspects of racing, and would never ever betray a confidence, however tempting it must have been when he was a leading journalist as well as legendary race-caller. His final call was the Hennessy won by Graham Bradley on the grey Suny Bay, and in the very next race I was fortunate enough to put on the O'Sullevan black and yellow silks and go out to ride his chaser Sounds Fyne, trained by the late Jimmy FitzGerald (great man, but no relation). If ever a result was

Temporary vantage point at Fakenham.

written in the heavens it was this one: Sounds Fyne took up the running at the last fence and I only had to drive him out to win cosily. The perfect result.

Of course, for many people the true spirit of jump racing is to be found not at the big tracks staging high-profile events and festivals, but at the small, so-called 'gaff' tracks which pepper the jump racing atlas – and while nowhere else will ever produce the buzz that Cheltenham does, I have to admit that I love those places.

The local feel which characterises the gaffs is nowhere felt as keenly as at **Fakenham**, where there's such a strong sense of the local community. Nicky Henderson sent plenty of horses there and I rode plenty of winners.

The circuit is barely a mile round and pretty tight, but the fences are fair – and again the times of races give the lie to the idea that it's an exceptionally fast course.

Admittedly Fakenham was a long way from home, but I had a very good record there, and no matter how long the journey, if you've had a winner the return drive absolutely flies by. If you haven't had a winner it drags – especially if you have another marathon drive in prospect the next day.

For all Fakenham's rural charms, there's nowhere on the racing map remotely like **Cartmel**. For one thing, the atmosphere is truly unique, with 20,000-odd locals and Lake District holiday-makers cramming in, most them with barbecues, to a race meeting which hardly ever attracts the best horses but regularly attracts the top jockeys – for the simple reason that they love its informality.

I can remember the first time I rode there. While nowadays the facilities for the jockeys at Cartmel are excellent, back then they were pretty primitive. We got changed in a sort of shed, and there was no sauna or anything fancy like that.

(To be fair to the old Cartmel, much grander tracks lacked saunas when I was starting out. I remember arriving at Aintree to ride a horse named Skinnhill, trained by Tim Thomson Jones, at 10 stone in the Topham Trophy over the Grand National fences, and asking fellow jockey Peter Niven where the sauna was. There isn't one, said Peter. So I had to revert to old but tried-and-tested methods. I put on my tracksuit and encased myself in a couple of bin-liners, went into the valets' drying room, turned on all the tumble driers and opened their doors, and ran up and down on the spot for thirty minutes to shed the three pounds I needed to lose. All that effort was not exactly rewarded: I nearly fell off Skinnhill at the first, and though we got round all that wasting was never going to be worth it.)

PREVIOUS SPREAD AND RIGHT: Cartmel – sharp, eccentric, unique, and the crowds have to be seen to be believed.

When I first walked round Cartmel I found myself thinking: What on earth is this? The racecourse is squeezed into the centre of Cartmel village, and the track runs along the side of a road before banking sharply left by a wall, then along the side of a deeply packed wood, then through the trees and past the end of people's gardens. You whizz round and round the circuit until – having jumped the last fence going away from the stands, which is a very curious sensation for spectators and jockeys alike – you turn left up a chute through the centre of the course towards the winning post.

Cartmel can be a very tricky course to ride, particularly if you're not good at counting. It's such a tight and eccentric circuit, which you go round and round before heading up the chute, that it's easy enough to lose count of how many times you've been round, and either keep

going when you should have turned in, or turn in prematurely – in which case there's absolutely no way back. You find yourself thinking in the back of your mind: Have we been twice round or three times? People will read this and think I'm mad, but every time I rode at Cartmel – and at Hexham, where there's also a finishing chute – I found myself thinking: Are we finishing this time? A little demon sitting on my shoulder was telling me to go on for another circuit, while another was urging me to turn up the chute now.

Yes, this sounds daft. How can a professional jockey be so careless as to forget how many times he's been round? How difficult can it be to count the number of fences you've jumped? I have to declare that I've never got it wrong, but plenty have, including senior and very experienced jockeys, and plenty more will.

Uttoxeter – bring your caravan!

The fact is that there are so many things happening in a jockey's brain during a race – how to get your horse jumping, how to save ground, how you're going, how the others are going – that if for one split second your brain goes cold then SHIT! PANIC STATIONS! – you've made a howler, and neither the stewards nor the betting public will be falling over themselves to show understanding.

I have a very soft spot for **Ludlow**, not just on account of its wonderful country atmosphere but because it's where I rode my first ever winner, Lover's Secret on 20 December 1988. Not the most glamorous venue nor the most glittering prize – the Tanners Sauvignon Conditional Jockeys' Selling Hurdle was worth £730.80 to the winner – but you never forget where you start.

I have a far less pleasant personal association with **Market Rasen**, as it was there that I broke my neck for the first time, on Celtic Boy in the 2005 Summer Plate. The form book states baldly, 'third last fence was omitted due to injured jockey' – and that was me, who had been buried at that fence on the first circuit.

I always found that third last at Market Rasen a tricky fence. As you come out of the back straight you suddenly go into a bit of a dip on the approach to the first of three fences in the straight, and it seems to claim an awful lot of victims. The first few times I rode there I never seemed to get over that fence, and it took me about two years to get it right.

There was a similar problem with one particular fence at **Fontwell Park** – the one at the top of the hill, before you go down towards the winning post. In my early days I just couldn't seem to get that one right. I didn't know whether to pop it, or go for a long stride, or what, and after a while it so bothered me that one day, as we were walking round before the start of a chase, I asked Richard Guest, a more experienced jockey than myself at the time, what was the best way to ride that fence, and I'll never forget his answer: 'Just shut your eyes!'

At the intersection on the Fontwell Park chase course, before the old stand was replaced: Yangtse-Kiang with jockey Granville Davies in August 1988.

This wasn't advice that I heeded to the letter, but I told myself to stop worrying and just treat that obstacle like any other fence – and from then on I rarely had a problem with it.

I did once, though, when riding Amtrak Express for Nicky Henderson. Amtrak Express was a small horse but a tremendously athletic jumper, and he tended to overjump, so that his nose would hit the ground first. One day in 1993 he absolutely buried me at that downhill fence – and then, to add injury to insult, threw out a foot as he was struggling to get up and caught me square on the bridge of my nose, smashing it into about fifteen pieces. I was taken to the medical room, where an old doctor told me – as if I needed telling – that I had broken my nose, and he'd try to manipulate it back into shape. As he did so the pain was so diabolical that I kept thinking I'd faint, and unsurprisingly he soon gave up and sent me off to hospital, where they started from scratch and reset the whole thing.

The day I resumed race-riding I was at Towcester, where I'd just got the leg-up on a runner trained by Kim Bailey – I've managed to erase the horse's name from my memory – when suddenly he threw his head back and whacked me in my freshly reconstructed nose, which was splattered all over my face.

Despite the eye-watering memory of that pain, I do think that Fontwell is a great track to ride around. Since the demise of jumping at Windsor, the chase course there is the only figure-of-eight circuit in Britain, which you would imagine would make it a course well suited to the nippy sort of horse. But contrary to appearances, Fontwell suits a front-runner, especially a good and accurate jumper.

And it's a tremendous course for racegoers. Standing by the fence just before the intersection offers an unparalleled opportunity to get close up and personal with the jump jockey experience, and wherever you are positioned at Fontwell, you're never far from the action.

My own first experience of getting close to the action was as a small child in the middle of the course at Killarney, where my mother used to take me with my brother and sister. Seeing horses up close when they're galloping and jumping was very special, and fired my interest in the game.

Towcester itself is a very different sort of circuit from Fontwell, and one where the basic requirements in a horse – and in a jockey – are stamina, stamina, and more stamina. It's the only track I've ever ridden round where going to the second last I've been leading but travelling so slowly that were I in fifth or sixth I'd certainly have pulled up. You can't believe there's anything still raising a gallop behind you, but you have to keep shoving away, just in case.

Unknown to those who have not ridden round it, Towcester has its own version of Becher's Brook: the open ditch after you've turned right beyond the stands. This fence has a huge drop on the landing side, and getting over it feels just like clearing Becher's.

The key to riding Towcester is to keep a little up your sleeve for that uphill slog from the bottom straight. The last ditch is three out, but it's still a hell of a long way home from there, and you have to keep your horse's revs up in order to jump cleanly, because if you let them pop the last two you're in grave danger of having them refuse, so slow are they going. It's not always a pretty sight to see knackered horses struggling up the hill, but Towcester is a track with great atmosphere and character, and I always welcomed its special challenges.

The same goes for **Plumpton**. I loved riding there, and over recent years the management have done wonders to improve the raceday experience, including great Family Days on Sundays, and an enclosure on the inside of the centre of the course where you can get very close to the action.

For many spectators the back straight at Plumpton seems an almost suicidally steep downhill, but it's not nearly as hairy as it looks, and on the whole this is a very fair track to ride. The key was always to get the fence at the top of the back straight right and then sprint down the hill to get your rivals at full stretch. You could

Plumpton – great atmosphere, and no wonder it's one of champ AP McCoy's favourite tracks. Here I'm on the left on Non So, about to beat Tom Doyle and Tidour in a novice chase in January 2004.

win or lose a race down that straight, though it has to be said that most experienced Plumpton jockeys – and nobody used to ride the place better than the indestructible Ray Goldstein – were alive to that ploy and wouldn't let the leader get too far ahead.

If Plumpton is a fairly straightforward course, the same cannot be said of **Bangor**. The two things which every dyed-in-the-wool jumping fan knows about Bangor are: (a) the course has no grandstand, and spectators get their view standing on the hill; and (b) it is near Wrexham, and nothing to do with the Bangor on the north Wales coast, as many a horsebox driver who has mis-programmed the SatNav has found to his cost.

I always found it a funny track to ride. You felt like you were turning all the time, and the final fence and hurdle are so close to the winning post that if your horse makes a mistake at the last there's very little opportunity to get back.

Sedgefield – a real jewel among the smaller courses.

Sedgefield is a long way from my usual stamping ground but it was a lucky track for me, and I rode ten winners there over the years. It's a demanding track, and the final hill is absolutely brutal – so much so that an awful lot of races there change complexion completely between the last fence or hurdle and the winning post. Horses are creatures of habit, and when they are tired they will naturally make for a place they know. Nor are they aware where the winning post is, so when they're faced with that grinding Sedgefield hill their natural instinct is to veer off right towards the stables, and a jockey has to be alert to that possibility.

At the other end of the country, Somerset, Devon and south Wales offer a variety of racecourses.

Ffos Las, deep in south-west Wales yet easily accessible from the M4, opened after I had retired from the saddle, but the boys who have ridden there have nothing but praise for the racing surface, the make-up of the fences, and the configuration of the course itself. Left-handed and flat with good long straights, they say it rides very similar to Newbury – and there aren't many more complimentary comments than that.

Riding at **Chepstow**, the other course in south Wales and home of the Welsh National, can be a very gruelling experience in heavy going, and it's not unusual to see the runners spread out like Sioux warriors as they come into the straight. For some reason you really have to select your trainers round there. Time after time the same trainers do very well, while some top-class trainers do significantly worse at Chepstow than at other courses.

Time was when you could easily pick up a few soft races at the West Country courses, but nowadays there's no such thing as a weak novice hurdle at Taunton, Exeter, Newton Abbot or Wincanton, as three of the most powerful yards in the country are

The water jump in front of the stands is just one of the appealing features of Perth.

down there, and you'd be hard pressed to find a race without a runner from the Paul Nicholls, Philip Hobbs or David Pipe stables.

Wincanton, Paul's local track, offers a very real test for a novice chaser, and the fences there are in my opinion the stiffest in the country. Indeed, as far as I'm concerned a horse who can jump round Wincanton can jump anywhere. They ought to put up a health warning at the entrance to Wincanton: 'Good horses only should race here.'

The two courses deepest into the West could hardly be more different. **Exeter** has a circuit two miles round, which makes it one of the longest in the country, but while it represents a stiff test for a horse, there's none fairer. **Newton Abbot**, on the other hand, is very tight, and you need a horse with good tactical pace there.

The Irish jumps tracks are just as varied in their shape, character and mood as the British, but the one event that stands out, in much the same way as the Cheltenham Festival stands out, is the great April meeting at **Punchestown**.

This five-day festival offers a similar fare of top-notch racing as Cheltenham, and features such contests as the Kerrygold Champion Chase, Punchestown Gold Cup, World Series Hurdle, Punchestown Champion Hurdle and Champion Four-year-old Hurdle. But the race which really engages the locals and intrigues the thousands of British visitors is the La Touche Cup, the famous cross-country race over 4 miles 3 furlongs, one of the most historic competitions in all jump racing.

I rode in the La Touche Cup, and it was an amazing experience – an exhilarating variation on the regular trade of a jump jockey. The course twists and turns and takes you over an astonishing variety of jumps, but the best moments of all are when you take the big bank. You jump up onto it, take one stride and then jump off, and to get that obstacle just right is every bit as exciting as soaring over Becher's Brook.

One trainer above all is a past master at preparing horses for the Punchestown cross-country course: Enda Bolger, who has won the La Touche Cup with astounding regularity, and has brought his genius to a wider audience with his runners in the cross-country races at Cheltenham. Horses trained by Enda seem to tackle the Punchestown banks even without thinking – for them, it's a simple case of hop, skip and off – and his record is simply unbelievable. The key to his success is that his cross-country performers have been educated all their lives by jumping the obstacles all round his farm, and the Punchestown course holds no fears whatsoever for them – they're just doing what comes naturally.

Of course, Punchestown is not only about the cross-country races, and at the Festival meeting in particular the racing is of a

FOLLOWING SPREAD: Riding over Ruby's Double, the big double bank at Punchestown, named after Ruby Walsh's grandfather.

31

OPPOSITE: Two of the delights of Irish racing: ABOVE, Killarney, BELOW, Bellewstown.

very high order indeed, with lots of Cheltenham Festival runners – winners as well as losers – competing for valuable and prestigious prizes.

The hurdles track at Punchestown is particularly quick, and can be a hair-raising experience for a jockey. Riding in a 25-runner handicap hurdle you're so tightly jammed in that you scarcely see a single flight. You've just got to hope that your horse has got his eyes open, because you'll be so crammed in like a sardine in that you won't be able to see a thing.

For an Irishman like me to come back to ride a winner at Punchestown was a dream come true.

With all its championship races, Punchestown in late April is a wonderfully enjoyable occasion, and with all that *craic* over five days of sport you need an iron constitution to get through it.

But for the big late-July meeting at **Galway**, which now lasts *seven days*, you need not just an iron constitution but an even stronger will, for if you get too tied up in the social side you're in serious trouble – or at least you are if you're a professional jockey expected to be on the ball and at the right weight the following day. The Galway Festival is essentially a week of partying punctuated by some very good racing – notably, of course, the Galway Plate, a handicap chase over 2¾ miles which invariably attracts a big field and can be a fierce betting race.

From the riding point of view Galway is a great track, though the run-in from the last fence feels very long, and sometimes a horse leading over the last can get lonely on that run to the line, and risks getting caught.

A lesser festival meeting in terms of the overall class of the sport, but certainly not lesser in terms of the *craic*, is the week-long meeting at **Listowel** in September. Traditionally this was a fixture at which the local farmers let their hair down after the rigours of the

harvest, but in truth it's just the excuse for one huge party – though to be fair, the Kerry National is a competitive race, and was won by Monty's Pass before he landed the 2003 Grand National. The track is very tight – and so, as the last race approaches, are many of the racegoers.

Leopardstown, in the Dublin suburbs, is one of the best racecourses in the world under both Flat and jumping codes, but – as with so many other courses – can look less testing to spectators than it really is, and the climb from the back straight to the last fence is much more uphill than it appears from the stands. You need a horse who can really jump, as the fences are big and testing, and it is no coincidence that the major chases here – the Lexus Chase over Christmas and the Hennessy in February – attract top horses: Best Mate, for instance, and special mention must be made of good old Beef Or Salmon, who never seemed to run to his true form in England but had a phenomenal record around Leopardstown, where he won the Lexus Chase and the Hennessy three times each.

Fairyhouse, home of the Irish Grand National on Easter Monday, is relatively flat but, as at Leopardstown, the fences are very stiff. There never seemed to be much give in them, with the result that hitting a Fairyhouse fence at full speed felt like hitting a wall at 30mph.

It would be invidious to single out more racecourses in Ireland, as I loved every Irish course at which I rode, whether in the Premier League with Punchestown or Leopardstown or a small country circuit like Roscommon.

Further afield, I loved the experience of riding at **Auteuil**, the track in central Paris which is to French jump racing – at least in terms of the concentration of major races – what Cheltenham is

to British. I twice rode there in the big four-year-old hurdle, and was immediately struck by the size of the place. Everything about Auteuil is large. The stands are massive – and very rarely filled – and the course itself is extraordinarily wide. There is just so much room, but the ground is usually so soft that the horses are almost going in up to their hocks.

British jumping fans of a certain age will always associate Auteuil with the truly unbelievable race in 1962 when Fred Winter and Mandarin – the gutsy little horse who earlier that year had won the Cheltenham Gold Cup – won the Grand Steeplechase de Paris, despite Mandarin's bit having snapped early in the race, leaving Fred with no means of steering round the notoriously difficult figure-of-eight steeplechase course. How Mandarin broke down close home, but still found the willpower to get up and win by a short head, is the stuff of jump racing legend (see page 216).

My own Auteuil experience was of the less challenging hurdles course, which is not figure-of-eight but the more orthodox oval round the outside. The hurdles themselves were much higher than ours but designed to be brushed through rather than cleared, and

Auteuil, with that tremendous chaser First Gold (centre) on the way to winning the Grand Steeplechase de Paris in 1998. (Jockey Thierry Doumen is wearing the colours of the Marquesa de Moratalla, who owned First Gold before he was sold to JP McManus.)

FOLLOWING SPREAD: Sheep may safely graze: out in the country at Chepstow.

a horse needed only get two feet or so off the ground in order to brush through the flimsy upper part.

Riding at Auteuil was quite an experience, but perhaps the most unusual racecourse I ever rode on was **Far Hills,** New Jersey.

In October 2001 I was called out of the blue by Jonathan Sheppard, the English-born trainer who has long dominated jump racing in the USA. I didn't know him at all at that stage, but he came straight to the point: Would I ride a horse named It's A Giggle for him in the Breeders' Cup Chase at Far Hills?

The Breeders' Cup has been the self-declared 'World Championships' of Flat racing since the mid-1980s, but I was only vaguely aware that the annual programme included a steeplechase. (Morley Street, one of the great English-trained hurdlers two decades ago, had won the race at Belmont Park in 1990.)

I accepted Jonathan's offer without a second thought, and was looking forward to the trip even more after I'd heard that Carl Llewellyn was also going out to ride in the race. Whatever happened to our horses, we'd have some fun along the way.

On the night we arrived, our fun was confined to a few beers in a gloomy bar where the bartender advised us that the nearest town was an hour and a half away, and those beers had made me a trifle heavy by the time I weighed myself the following day – the day of the Breeders' Cup Steeplechase. Never mind, I thought: I'll get to the track early and have a good sweat in the sauna.

When we arrived at the racecourse, it was time for a rethink. Not only was there no sauna, there was no changing room, no shower or any other facility – in fact there was just a tent for the jockeys, as there were tents for all other standard racecourse uses. Far Hills was not really a racecourse at all in the sense that I had imagined it would be, and once I realised that I was able to enjoy the experience. Although I thought that I'd been booked just for the Jonathan Sheppard horse in the Breeders' Cup Steeplechase, it turned out that the racecard had me down to ride four others. I managed to get out of getting the leg up on a three-year-old having its first ever race (I've never been one to duck a challenge, but that would have been foolhardy), but I reluctantly agreed to ride another at 10st 2lb, when I had to put up 8lb overweight.

The racecourse was a bit like an English or Irish point-to-point course, with only very basic facilities for racegoers, and the track was riding considerably firmer than we would have considered safe for jump racing. When I mentioned this to the locals, they declared it perfect ground.

But the really amazing aspect of Far Hills was the size of the crowd: at least 60,000 people sitting round with their picnics and barbecues – Cartmel meets Larkhill – and generating an atmosphere the like of which I have never encountered.

It's A Giggle could finish only fifth in the Breeders' Cup Chase – Carl (or 'The Welsh', as he was known in the weighing room) was fourth on Pinkie Swear – but I managed to cajole the horse on which I had to put up the 8lb overweight to get his nose in front on the line, to give me my one and only winner in the USA.

That was great, but it was the whole trip which I'll never forget – and the chance to ride at one of the most unusual jumps tracks in the world. Jumping in the USA has a wholly different feel from in Britain or Ireland but, as Far Hills proved, it can generate just as much buzz.

Apologies if I've failed to mention your favourite course. Every single track has its particular fans among racegoers and among jockeys, and – as I said at the head of this chapter – as far as jumping courses are concerned, variety is very much the spice of life.

26

THE GRAND NATIONAL

PREVIOUS SPREAD: Becher's first time round in the 2009 John Smith's Grand National, with 100-1 winner Mon Mome (no. 15) landing steeply enough to puff out Liam Treadwell's cheeks.

The Cheltenham Festival forms the annual focal point of the jumping season, but there's no question that the single race which transcends the sport, which is guaranteed to make front-page as well as back-page news – the 'race which stops the nation', if you like – is the Grand National.

Every year in early April the focus of the sporting world is on Aintree racecourse, which in terms of surroundings could hardly be more different from the glorious backdrop of Cheltenham's Cleeve Hill. Aintree is an unprepossessing suburb of Liverpool, very close to where the end of the M57 motorway meets the end of the M58, flat terrain as far as the eye can see. Not even the proudest Liverpudlian would claim that the setting has special scenic qualities.

But as with every other aspect of this most historic of races, the Grand National rises above its surroundings, and – as we saw on pages 40–43 – the three-day National meeting has a character all its own. The racing itself is fantastic, the Ladies of Liverpool *en masse* are an unforgettable sight, and with the building of the Earl of Derby Stand and Lord Sefton Stand in the last few years, and the re-siting and upgrading of the parade ring and winner's enclosure, the facilities for racegoers are first-rate. For jockeys, there is a huge buzz over all three days, though the atmosphere is much more relaxed than at the Cheltenham Festival, where every rider is so desperate to ride a winner that tension fills the changing room. And on National day there is a special glow on the faces of the forty fortunate enough to have a ride in the big race.

As a contest the Grand National is, quite simply, unlike any other. Run over 4½ miles, it is the longest race in the calendar, and its thirty fences, quite different in their make-up from the fences at other racecourses, not only form a unique challenge for horse and

A rush of pure adrenaline: at the eleventh fence on Rough Quest (no. 7) in the 1996 Martell Grand National.

rider but have a magic all their own with household names like Becher's Brook, Valentine's, the Chair and the Canal Turn.

The race invariably attracts a large field – a maximum of forty these days, on safety grounds – and is run at an unremitting speed, so it is not surprising that for any jockey, top flight or journeyman, riding in the National is a very special experience indeed. I was fortunate enough to sample the heady elixir of winning on Rough Quest in 1996, and although it seems I'll always have to live with my post-race assertion to the BBC's Des Lynam that 'After that, sex will be an anti-climax', that remark at least shows that my euphoria was genuine!

A major element in that feeling was the realisation that I had joined a very select band of riders. Many champion jump jockeys never won the race – including Terry Biddlecombe, Josh Gifford, Ron Barry, Stan Mellor, Jonjo O'Neill (who never even got round), John Francome and Peter Scudamore – and to join the special group who have won was a wonderfully satisfying feeling.

There has been some dispute among racing historians regarding exactly when the race was first run, but the most favoured year is 1839, not least because the winner that year was a horse with the perfect name for a Grand National runner: Lottery. By the end of the

Calm before the storm: 7am on Grand National morning.

nineteenth century the National was enjoying a unique place in the public regard, and the turn of the twentieth century saw the career of one of the most remarkable National horses of all. Manifesto ran in the race no fewer than eight times between 1895 and 1904, usually carrying huge weights: he won in 1897 and 1899, finished third three times (on the last occasion at the age of fifteen) and fourth once, and his final appearance in the race was as a 16-year-old: he finished eighth.

That was hard act to follow, but throughout the twentieth century and the first decade of the twenty-first, the Grand National has never lost its ability to produce remarkable stories, among them:

- **1928**: 100-1 shot Tipperary Tim and the remounted Billy Barton are the only two finishers after the great Easter Hero had caused chaos by getting stuck on top of the Canal Turn – then an open ditch – on the first circuit;
- **1934**: five-time Cheltenham Gold Cup winner Golden Miller becomes the only horse ever to win the Gold Cup and Grand National in the same year;

- **1938**: 17-year-old Bruce Hobbs, later a leading trainer, wins by a head on the tiny entire horse Battleship, becoming the youngest ever National-winning jockey;
- **1953, 1954 and 1955**: Vincent O'Brien, later considered the greatest Flat trainer of all, wins three consecutive Nationals with three different horses – Early Mist, Royal Tan and Quare Times – an extraordinary feat;
- **1956**: the sensational collapse of Devon Loch, described below on pages 177–9;
- **1967**: the Foinavon farce – see pages 179–81;
- **1973-77**: the age of Red Rum, who in five consecutive Nationals is never worse than second, overhauling Crisp to win the heart-rending 1973 race (pages 181–5); finishing second to L'Escargot (only horse apart from Golden Miller to win the Cheltenham Gold Cup and Grand National) in 1975 and Rag Trade in 1976; then landing an historic third National when beating Churchtown Boy in 1977;
- **1981**: the emotionally charged victory of Bob Champion and Aldaniti – see pages 185–7;
- **1983**: Corbiere makes Jenny Pitman the first lady trainer of a Grand National winner;

The Ladies of Liverpool add an extra dimension to National Day.

The 1993 false starts fiasco, with Richard Dunwoody looking about to be garotted on Wont Be Gone Long.

- **1993**: fiasco – two false starts and the 'race', won by John White on Esha Ness, is declared void;
- **1997**: an IRA bomb warning causes the mass evacuation of the stands and the cancellation of the National – which is run two days later on the Monday, with Lord Gyllene a brilliant winner;
- **2001**: Red Marauder slogs through bottomless conditions to beat Smarty – and the only other finishers are Blowing Wind and 2000 winner Papillon, both of whom have been remounted;
- **2010**: AP McCoy, greatest jump jockey of all, finally wins the Grand National at his fifteenth attempt – on Don't Push It, owned by his patron JP McManus and trained by Jonjo O'Neill: see pages 187–91.

The Grand National is custom-built to provide drama, excitement, and – win or lose – heroics from horse and jockey. There's just nothing like it in the world.

THE COURSE

What gives the Grand National its special quality and special resonance is the course itself, almost two complete circuits featuring names known to millions outside racing: Becher's Brook, two words which have entered the English language as a term for an obstacle particularly difficult to get over; Valentine's Brook; the Chair; the Melling Road; the Elbow. And, uniquely for a British racecourse, the fences are constructed not in the standard form of birch packed into a wooden frame, but of hawthorn stakes dressed with spruce, gorse and fir. (Until 1961 the fences had no sloping apron on the take-off side, which made them even more daunting than they are now.)

For jockeys, that feeling that the National is a race unto itself is augmented by the immediate build-up. Shortly before the riders are due to leave the weighing room, a group consisting of the stewards, the starter, the clerk of the course and the flagman come in for the traditional pre-Grand National briefing, which goes along the lines of: 'Be sensible … Please obey the starter … Don't go too fast to the

The 1997 bomb scare.

37

first fence … The world is watching … We want a trouble-free race … Best of luck to you all.' It would be unfair to compare the response to this annual warning too closely to the reaction of seasoned airline passengers when the pre-flight safety message is being made, and it does contain one vital piece of information: the colours by which the jockeys are to recognise the official flags which will be used in the event of a problem, and which must be obeyed.

OPPOSITE: The Grand National start in 2003.

The new weighing room at Aintree allows for the National jockeys to make a semi-ceremonial exit before the race, down the steps to the winner's podium, where they pose for the official pre-race photo, and this all adds to the sense of theatre in the run-up to the big race. After a few nervous words with connections in the parade ring, getting legged up into the saddle tends to settle you down: now it's time to concentrate 100 per cent on the race.

Runners sort themselves into racecard order, parade in front of the jam-packed stands, turn and canter beyond the start to take a look at the first fence, and then return to the starting area at the beginning of the long straight which takes in the first six fences.

Tension can get to jockeys and horses through all these preliminaries, and it's a huge relief when the starter finally calls you to make a line.

There have been various shenanigans at the National start over the last few years – notably, of course, the two false starts in 1993 which led to the race being declared void, an occasion I remember very vividly, not least because I was not there. I was due to ride Just So in the big race and strongly fancied my chances. A sound jumper suited by extreme distances, he was made-to-measure for the National – as he was to prove when runner-up to Miinnehoma the following year – but was withdrawn on the morning of the race. I was gutted, but changed my plans and drove sharply down to Hereford, where I'd managed to get a couple of rides at short

On their way: the 2007 John Smith's Grand National field crossing the Melling Road on the run to the first fence.

notice. After the fourth race at Hereford the jockeys settled down in the weighing room to watch the National on television, all of us mightily envious of our colleagues lining up for the world's biggest steeplechase. That envy rapidly turned to horror, and then relief that we weren't there and part of the farcical goings-on.

After all the ratcheting up of tension during the pre-prelims, it's a great relief when you're finally on your way and heading off on the long run towards the first fence, about a quarter of a mile from the start.

Over the years there has been a good deal of debate about whether the best line to take in the National is on the inside, middle or outside of the course. In the old days, going up the inner was a very high-risk strategy, as the drop on landing over Becher's Brook was significantly steeper on the inside, but nowadays the landing side has been levelled out – though the drop still makes it a very trappy fence – so the risk of tipping up has been significantly decreased.

I always thought that the middle to outside of the course was the sensible line to take, as things tend to get more congested up the inner, and I wanted as far as possible to give my horse a good look at each fence and not get bustled about too much.

With so many horses and jockeys so fired up, the run to the first fence can be a pretty hectic affair, and the first itself is a crucial moment in the race. Many horses are jumping these fences for the first time, and a jockey can usually tell straight away whether the first-timer will love or hate the experience: if love, you're in for a real thrill; if hate, you're in for an uncomfortable few minutes or a very early exit. My first ever Grand National ride was Tinryland in 1995, and he got only as far as the first – a desperately deflating experience, but what happened with Rough Quest the following year made up for it. And it's not only Aintree newcomers who can be caught out by the first: Aldaniti, whose famous victory in 1981 is described later, fell at the first the following year. In 1951 twelve runners – a third of the entire field – came to grief at the first, while in 1929 no fewer than 66 runners started the race, and there was not a single casualty at the first.

As well as being built in a way different from orthodox steeplechase fences, the National fences are noticeably wider from take-off to landing, and if your horse meets the first long and clears it well – as did Rough Quest – you can start to relax a little and get into a rhythm.

FOLLOWING SPREAD: Becher's Brook first time round in the 2007 John Smith's Grand National. Winner Silver Birch (Robbie Power, no. 30) is just behind the leaders.

15
3
25
2

6&22
BECHER'S
BROOK
10in Fence

The second fence is similar to the first – a nothing fence really, but of huge personal resonance to myself: it was on L'Ami at the second in the 2008 Grand National that I suffered the fall which ended my riding career.

The third is noticeably higher than the first two and has a 6ft-wide ditch yawning on the take-off side. The biggest fence on the course is the fifteenth, the Chair, but many jockeys consider the third even more challenging, as it's so early in the race that you might not have settled down properly, and from take-off to landing seems a huge distance.

Two more plain fences, and then comes Becher's Brook, so named because it was here that in the first Grand National in 1839 Captain Martin Becher parted company from his horse Conrad and landed in the brook. The approach to this most famous of all Grand National fences is marked by a low hedge on the inside rail, and

Canal Turn first time round, 2008.

the fence itself is at a slight angle to the course. It measures 4ft 10in on the take-off side but 7ft on the landing side, and that drop is the crucial aspect of Becher's. Although some of the first five fences have minor drops on the landing side, the Becher's drop is of a wholly different order. Your horse will not be expecting it, and if he has even slightly over-jumped he risks crumpling on landing.

The first time you ever jump Becher's it's like the downward lurch of a roller-coaster – you feel you're leaving your stomach behind you – and every time after that the feeling is similar, though the more familiar the sensation becomes, the more you get to enjoy it.

By the fence after Becher's a good National horse has learned enough about the hazards of the obstacles to start becoming careful at each jump, and with a quirkiness characteristic of the course, the fence immediately after the most difficult obstacle is effectively the easiest. But there is a warning in its name, as the seventh, reached

very soon after Becher's by a slight left-hand turn, is the Foinavon Fence, so named following the chaos there in 1967, described on pages 179–81. This is the smallest fence on the circuit and these days rarely causes much trouble, but the next – the eighth – is the Canal Turn, one of the most extraordinary obstacles in the sport. Immediately on landing you veer sharp left – in the old days, if you didn't make that turn you ended up in the canal! – to face the next run of fences. Naturally the way to approach the Canal Turn is to pull out wide on the approach and jump the fence at a 45-degree angle.

From the Canal Turn back to the Melling Road is a stretch which is wonderful to ride: completely straight, and with lots of room affording you plenty of time to line up your horses for four fences which, while big, are beautifully made and a joy to ride over. Following the Canal Turn comes Valentine's Brook, the lesser sibling of Becher's (though it's the same brook) and named after a horse who in 1840 tried to pull himself up here and made a sort of pirouette to the landing side and went on to finish third.

The tenth is a plain fence, the eleventh an open ditch, the twelfth a fence with a ditch on the landing side – and then it's back across

Valentine's Brook 2002: Sir Robert Ogden's grey Kingsmark (Ruby Walsh), who finished fourth, ahead of his other runner Ad Hoc (Paul Carberry), brought down four fences out.

the Melling Road and a gradual left turn towards the thirteenth and fourteenth fences. The run down from the Canal Turn is quiet, as there are not many spectators along the fence on the outside of the course, but as you turn to approach the thirteenth you start hearing the noise of the crowd in the stands, which ratchets up the excitement. The thirteenth and fourteenth are both straightforward enough, but then the course narrows as you come to the Chair – so called because it was here that, generations ago, the 'distance judge' sat on his chair to record the finishers.

The official dimensions of the Chair are that the fence is 5ft 2in – highest on the course – and the ditch preceding it is 6ft wide, but what makes it especially fearsome is that at 15 yards from outside to inside, it has significantly less width than the other fences. The key to getting over it in one piece – or at least still connected with your partner (see pages 18 –19 for the alternative) – is to get the horse back on his hocks and take off as close as possible to the guard rail.

Next comes the water jump, right in front of the stands and straightforward enough to negotiate, and then there's an opportunity to get a breather into your horse as you set out on the second circuit.

The traditional advice to Grand National jockeys was to 'hunt round on the first circuit and start riding your race on the second', and that applies just as much nowadays. Across the Melling Road and approaching what was the first fence and is now the seventeenth, you start to become more aware of the horses around you: who is going well and who is struggling, who is enjoying the jumping experience and who is resenting the Aintree fences. An additional hazard by now is the number of loose horses whose herd instinct is keeping them galloping along with their fellows, and the sheer unpredictability of what a loose horse might do is a big problem for all surviving jockeys, some of whom are just beginning to think they're in with a real chance.

Red Rum and Brian Fletcher airborne over second Becher's in 1973 – but still some thirty lengths behind Crisp. (See pages 181–5.)

After second Becher's the race is really taking shape, and the stretch from the Canal Turn second time round makes everybody's water tingle. The winner is almost certainly among the leaders here, but the fences, by now surrounded by a debris of fir, gorse and spruce from the first circuit, still need jumping cleanly, and the complexion of the race can change in an instant. In this section of the National, maintaining your rhythm is absolutely paramount,

OPPOSITE: The last fence in the 2010 John Smith's Grand National: Don't Push It and AP McCoy shade Black Apalachi and Denis O'Regan.

as making a mistake over these fences takes more out of your horse than mistakes on other courses, and at this point it is vital to conserve your horse's energy – and your own.

Being in contention as you come round towards what is now the 29th and second last fence is an experience in itself, but there's still plenty more of the race to unfold, as Aintree keeps its most demanding trick until after the last. The run-in from the last is over a quarter of a mile long, and for tired horses and jockeys that can be a real slog. The Elbow, the point where finishers go right to avoid facing the Chair again, can cause problems as one horse tries to get up the inner to gain the benefit of the rail, and for the jockey in front the final 200 yards seem like miles. But if he reaches the post still in front his life will never be the same again.

History made: a third Grand National for Red Rum as Tommy Stack brings the Liverpool legend home in 1977.

THE UNFORGETTABLES

The Grand National story is festooned with incredible stories and sensational outcomes. In a sense every single running is unforgettable, but here are five etched more deeply than most into National history.

DEVON LOCH, 1956

Next time you think your horse an unlucky loser, dig out the history books and remind yourself what happened in the 1956 Grand National, a race so notorious that the name of Devon Loch, a horse who failed to finish, has become synonymous with the idea of defeat snatched from the jaws of victory.

Owned by Queen Elizabeth the Queen Mother, whose involvement in jump racing from the late 1940s was hugely influential in bringing the sport to a wider audience, and trained by Peter Cazalet, Devon Loch was ridden in the National by Dick Francis, one of the most popular jump jockeys of the day and champion in the 1953-4 season.

By the Canal Turn second time round Devon Loch was close behind the leaders and travelling well, and then found himself in the lead at the fence after Valentine's Brook. At the last fence he was still clear and going easily, and as he set off up the run-in well ahead of ESB, the crowd started going wild at the prospect of a royal victory in the National.

Watch Devon Loch coming round the elbow still galloping powerfully and then bearing down inexorably on the winning post, and you're deep into 'What Happened Next?' territory. In this case what happened next is best described in his jockey's autobiography, *The Sport of Queens*:

In one stride he was bounding smoothly along, a poem of controlled motion; in the next, his hind legs stiffened and refused to function. He fell flat on his belly, his limbs splayed out sideways and backwards in unnatural angles, and when he stood up he could hardly move … The rhythm was shattered, the dream was over, and the race was lost.

ESB and jockey Dave Dick galloped past the immobilised Devon Loch to record an astonishing victory from Gentle Moya, and after a short while the Queen Mother's horse was led away, apparently sound, while the inconsolable jockey trudged off the course.

It was the most extraordinary moment that jump racing has ever seen, and no one has ever been able to explain why it had happened. While many people thought that Devon Loch had suffered some muscular cramp – an understandable explanation, given the distance of the Grand National at 4½ miles – Dick Francis's own view was that the horse was scared by the wall of noise, which he described in this way:

I have never in my life heard such a noise. It rolled and lapped around us, buffeting and glorious, the enthusiastic expression of love for the royal family and delight in seeing the royal horse win.

Obviously Dick's opinion has to be given more credence than the views of others who were not, as it were, in the driving seat at the time. But the more I look at that incident – and I have done so a hundred times on YouTube – the more convinced I become that the horse was trying to jump an imaginary obstacle. The slide occurred right by the water jump, and Devon Loch pricks his ears and takes off, as he would if jumping. Maybe he was distracted by the tunnel of noise which Dick mentions into seeing a non-existent obstacle ahead of him, but in any case his movements strongly suggest that he was jumping – and then, when he realises that there is nothing to jump, he belly-flops in confusion.

Dick Francis, a wonderfully humble and unassuming man who sadly died in February 2010, made no bones of the fact that losing on Devon Loch in such a manner made him far more famous than winning would have done. When he retired from the saddle not long after that Aintree horror, he became a journalist and then, of course, the writer of hugely successful thrillers. The millions of devoted readers who lap up his novels probably have a skewed notion of just how much skulduggery there is in racing, but there is nothing in any of those novels quite as sensational as what really happened in the 1956 Grand National.

FOINAVON, 1967

Foinavon's Grand National overturned all racing logic: he won because he was so hopelessly behind at the time of the race's defining moment. His win beggared belief, and for me it still does, but it's part of Grand National folklore.

Originally owned by Arkle's owner Anne, Duchess of Westminster – and like Arkle named after a mountain on her Scottish estates – Foinavon proved so impossibly lazy as a racehorse that he was sold for 2,000 guineas and joined small-time trainer John Kempton's yard in Compton, Berkshire.

Earlier in the 1966-67 season Foinavon had finished a remote fourth behind Dormant and the stricken Arkle in the King George VI Chase, and three weeks before the National had finished last in the Cheltenham Gold Cup at 500-1, so his National starting price of 100-1 was hardly generous.

The nine-year-old was ridden in the National by John Buckingham as his trainer, who usually rode the horse, could not do the weight of 10 stone, and it is a measure of connections' confidence that owner Cyril Watkins stayed at home to watch the race on television and Kempton himself went to ride at Worcester.

After a fierce early pace, by the start of the second circuit Foinavon was getting further and further behind, and approaching second Becher's was pretty well out with the washing. The leaders, accompanied by two loose horses, swept over Becher's and made for the 23rd fence – at which point the loose Popham Down, who had parted company with his rider at the first and was now with the leaders on the inside of the course, suddenly, a stride before the fence, slammed on the brakes, veered right and slammed into Rutherfords, setting off a concertina effect which in seconds had brought most of the field to a shuddering, chaotic halt. The great Irish commentator Michael O'Hehir was covering that phase of

Carnage at the 23rd fence.

the race for BBC television, and produced one of the all-time great pieces of sporting commentary: 'Rondetto has fallen, Princeful has fallen, Norther has fallen, Kirtle Lad has fallen, The Fossa has fallen, there's a right pile-up …'

Some horses managed to get to the landing side but without their jockeys, while some jockeys were shot to the landing side without their horses. Gorse was flying in all directions. It was total chaos – and then Foinavon ambled into view, John Buckingham picked his spot towards the outside of the course, clambered over and was away. He cleared the Canal Turn, Valentine's and the remaining five fences in glorious isolation, and although Josh Gifford on the favourite Honey End made up a huge amount of the deficit, Foinavon kept going to win by 15 lengths.

The luckiest winner in National history? Perhaps – but Foinavon won because he was in the right place at the right time, and luck plays an important part in any Grand National. Like it or not, his name is on the roll of honour – and that's that.

CRISP and RED RUM, 1973

The 1973 Grand National was such an extraordinary race that every time I watch it again, I think the outcome will be different. Sadly – at least for the many devoted followers of the great Australian chaser Crisp – it isn't, and I still can't really believe it.

Crisp had come from Australia three years earlier to join the great jockey-turned-trainer Fred Winter, in whose charge he had won several races, notably the Two-Mile Champion Chase (now the Queen Mother Champion Chase) at the 1971 Cheltenham Festival by 25 lengths. In March 1973 he had finished third in the Champion Chase before heading for Aintree and the National. The Liverpool showpiece was run over a distance 2½ miles longer than the Cheltenham two-miler, but Crisp's sheer class and brilliant jumping would stand him in good

Crisp (Richard Pitman) in glorious isolation at second Becher's, and seeming impossible to catch.

stead, and with Richard Pitman in the saddle he started joint favourite at 9-1 despite carrying top weight of 12st.

The other joint-favourite was an eight-year-old scrapper named Red Rum, ridden by Brian Fletcher and carrying 23lb less than top-weight Crisp. In his first ever race Red Rum had been ridden by Paul Cook to dead-heat in a two-year-old seller at Liverpool the day before the Foinavon Grand National, and he had been on the go ever since, having a succession of trainers before ending up in Ginger McCain's yard behind his second-hand car showroom in Southport, where a training routine based on gallops along the beach worked wonders on Red Rum's dodgy legs. By the time of the 1973 National the compact bay gelding was one of the best handicap chasers in the north.

It was expected that Crisp would take a prominent role from early in the race, and over the early fences he was right up there in the front rank. At Becher's first time round he was vying for the lead with Grey Sombrero, but by Valentine's he was clear, and from then on gradually increased his advantage. Richard knew better than try to restrain this great front-runner, and by the Chair he was some twenty lengths to the good. It was an astounding sight, but it got better and better.

Going out for the second circuit he still had an enormous lead, and none of the others seemed to be making any ground – though Brian Fletcher had moved Red Rum up into a remote second place. Crisp soared over the 19th, the big open ditch, causing Julian Wilson on BBC television to exclaim, 'I can't remember a horse so far ahead in the Grand National at this stage!', and sailed over second Becher's. He was thirty lengths clear, producing what was already one of the most sensational Grand National performances ever. Over the Canal Turn and Valentine's, five to jump, four, three – and then he turned towards the stands, still apparently full of running. The more sharp-eyed in the crowd saw that Red Rum, though still some thirty lengths adrift, was even further clear of the remaining runners and might even be getting a tiny bit closer, but surely he'd never get to Crisp. At the second last the Australian was ten lengths up, but his stride was shortening – surely the weight was beginning to tell – and Richard's anxious glance over his shoulder gave Brian Fletcher some encouragement. At the last fence Crisp still held a big lead but his stride was shortening and Red Rum was closing relentlessly, and as Richard and his rapidly weakening partner started up the endless run-in it was simply a question of whether he would last home. Richard gave him a smack with the whip down the right, Crisp swerved to the left, Richard yanked him back on course – and all the time Red Rum was getting closer and closer. At the Elbow it still looked as if Crisp would make it, but he was completely drained, and Red Rum was now an unstoppable force. With Crisp barely able to raise a canter, a few yards from the

The shadow of the post – and Red Rum collars Crisp.

post Red Rum got his nose in front. The winning margin was three quarters of a length, and the time of the race beat the previous record by nearly twenty seconds.

It's often forgotten that Red Rum and Crisp met again the following November, in a two-horse race at level weights at Doncaster. Crisp won that contest easily. There was never really any question that he was by far the better horse – the Grand National weights indicated that – but their relative merit was not the point anyway.

Crisp never ran again in the Grand National, while Red Rum went on to become the greatest National horse of all, winning off top weight in 1974, finishing runner-up to L'Escargot in 1975 and to Rag Trade in 1976, and then winning for an unparalleled third time in 1977, when ridden by Tommy Stack, who had been one of the horse's early trainers and had taken over the ride from Brian Fletcher before the 1976 National.

That 1977 victory was one of the iconic moments of jump racing history, but for sheer brilliance and undiluted drama, nothing can beat the 1973 race.

It was unbelievable. Look it up on YouTube – but have a hankie ready before you press 'Play'.

ALDANITI, 1981

Although I can remember my mother telling me all about Red Rum when he won his third National – I was nearly seven years old at the time – the first running of which I have a strong memory was the 1981 race, which produced a result written in the stars.

Bob Champion was one of Britain's leading jump jockeys when in the summer of 1979 he was diagnosed as having testicular cancer, with a lengthy and horrible course of chemotherapy the alternative to death within less than a year. Throughout his long and arduous treatment, Bob's spirit was sustained by the prospect of returning to ride for his guv'nor Josh Gifford, who had assured him that his position as stable jockey would remain open for him, and in particular the prospect of riding Aldaniti in the Grand National.

Aldaniti, owned by ship-broker Nick Embiricos, was himself something of a crock, having suffered tendon strain and then, when recovered from that setback, being sidelined again after chipping two bones in a pastern – and he suffered a further setback when breaking down in a race in November 1979.

Bob Champion returned to the saddle in August 1980 – 'Hail Champion the Wonder Horseman', trumpeted the *Sporting Life* headline – and the following February saw Aldaniti's return to the fray: he won a valuable race at Ascot, and the impossible dream of winning the Grand National under Champion seemed on the cards, so long as his fragile legs remained sound.

Get out the Kleenex – as Bob Champion and Aldaniti take the last fence ahead of Royal Mail (Philip Blacker), who finished third, while John Thorne (striped sleeves) on runner-up Spartan Missile is getting closer.

Aldaniti started second favourite for the 1981 Grand National, preferred in the betting market only by Spartan Missile, the great hunter-chaser who had twice won the Fox Hunters' Chase over the National fences and was ridden by 54-year-old John Thorne.

After making mistakes at the first two fences, Aldaniti settled down and started to enjoy himself. Coming past the stands at the end of the first circuit he was firmly in the front rank, and by second Becher's – where he turned in a prodigious leap – he had a definite lead. From then on it was simply a matter of Bob keeping him in the tremendous rhythm he had built up. The well-fancied Royal Mail looked like making a serious race of it until hitting the second last, leaving Aldaniti to jump the last with a definite lead and keep up his relentless gallop all the way to the line, where he passed the post four lengths clear of Spartan Missile, who had made up a good deal of ground in the closing stages without ever threatening to spoil the fairy tale.

No single race ever had a better outcome than the 1981 Grand National, as it inspired the foundation in 1983 of the Bob Champion Cancer Trust, which over the years has raised millions of pounds for cancer research. There was even a film made about this heart-warming story: *Champions* starred John Hurt as Bob Champion and Edward Woodward as Josh Gifford, but in truth the fictionalised version could hardly be more moving than the real thing. Who could not be moved by Bob's summing up of the 1981 National in his autobiography?

> *I rode this race for all the patients in hospital. And all the people who look after them. My only wish is that my winning shows them that there is always hope, and all battles can be won.*

DON'T PUSH IT and AP MCCOY, 2010

I should declare my interest: AP McCoy is one of my very best mates. He is also a rider of incomparable skill and determination who has taken riding over jumps to wholly new levels, but until 10 April 2010 there was a glaring gap in his record. He had never won the Grand National.

He'd had fourteen previous tries, starting back in 1995, and he'd had some pretty grisly experiences along the way. He failed to get round in his first five attempts (including a first-fence fall in

1998). He twice finished third on Blowing Wind, and is convinced he should have won on that horse in 2001, when Red Marauder slogged through impossible conditions to win: Blowing Wind was flattened by a loose horse early on the second circuit, and AP remounted. In 2005 he and Clan Royal had a five-length lead going down the outside towards second Becher's when the loose horses Merchants Friend and Take The Stand decided at the last moment not to jump the fence and swerved left, taking Clan Royal right across to the inside rail and giving AP no chance of staying in the saddle. After such experiences, he could have been forgiven for rating the National his bogey race.

During the run-up to the 2010 race there did not seem to be too much prospect of AP breaking his National duck, and it was only a few days before that he announced that he would be riding Don't Push It rather than Can't Buy Time. Both horses were owned by his boss JP McManus and trained by Jonjo O'Neill, but neither seemed to have a major chance.

In his last outing Don't Push It had finished tailed off in a hurdle race at the Cheltenham Festival, and although he had some very useful earlier form as a chaser, on the morning of the race he stood at 33-1 or so in the market. When the on-course betting on the National started in earnest, however, the weight of public money seemed to be willing AP to win at last, and a flood of bets brought Don't Push It down to 10-1 joint favourite with Big Fella Thanks.

The shape of the race is easily told: Don't Push It made steady progress throughout the second circuit, was close behind the leaders at second Becher's, took a narrow advantage over Black Apalachi going to the last and galloped on to finish five lengths clear. But it was what happened afterwards which made this one of the greatest of all Grand Nationals, as winning the race almost visibly lifted a vast weight off AP's shoulders. Giving way to a rare

OPPOSITE: Caption hardly necessary ...

JOHNSMITH'S

The 'wuss' returns.

moment of emotion, he described himself as 'a big wuss' for being so overcome by winning the National at last, and added: 'It means everything to me to win the Grand National. I've won lots of big races and I'm supposed to be a good jockey, but not to win the Grand National would be a bit of a negative on the cv. Everyone knows about the National, so from a public point of view to win the biggest race in the world means everything. At least I can feel now that I've done all right.' And for me, AP's most telling remark in the post-race euphoria was about his little daughter: 'Now Eve can be proud of her Daddy.'

This was the perfect result: a first National for AP; a first National for JP McManus, who had owned no fewer than 33 runners in the race before the 2010 running and had been such a magnificent supporter of the sport; and a first National for Jonjo O'Neill, who had such an unfortunate record in the race as a jockey – he never got further than the Canal Turn in seven attempts – and had gone close as a trainer when JP-owned Clan Royal was beaten three lengths by Amberleigh House in 2004.

For all that, this was very much AP's day, and his reaction to winning was as good an illustration as you could get of the sheer magic of the race.

Some wuss!

HEROES

PREVIOUS SPREAD: First Gold and AP McCoy (left) with Graham Lee and Grey Abbey in the Betfair Bowl at Aintree, 2005.

Every sport has its stars, and the history of jump racing is crowded with heroes – and heroines – whose achievements are at the heart of its appeal. Here are just a few of my own nominations for jump racing superstardom – and, in some cases, immortality. Some are household names; others unknown outside racing.

Pride of place naturally goes to the horses, the true stars of the sport – and where better to start than with the four undisputed greats whose achievements are recognised by their statues at Cheltenham racecourse?

In chronological order, that quartet of immortals consists of Golden Miller, Arkle, Dawn Run and Best Mate – but with all respect to supporters of the other three, the brightest star in the entire history of jump racing has to be the horse known simply as 'Himself'.

When **Arkle** was put down in May 1970 at the age of thirteen, I was just three weeks old, but thanks to the wonders of YouTube and the various DVDs about Himself, I've been able to watch many of his races. Wow!

His record was simply astonishing. Between November 1962 and December 1966 he ran twenty-six times over fences and won twenty-two, including the Gold Cup in 1964 (when he beat the previous year's winner Mill House in one of the most famous races of all time, described on pages 82–5 of this book), 1965 (beating Mill House again) and 1966. He won the Hennessy Gold Cup twice, the Leopardstown Chase three times, the Whitbread, Irish National and King George VI Chase. Timeform described him as 'as close to unbeatable as any horse is ever likely to be.'

He wasn't literally unbeatable, but there were solid excuses for the four times he was defeated in chases, the fourth of which

OPPOSITE: If God were a horse, He'd be Arkle – seen here with regular partner Pat Taaffe before the 1965 Hennessy Gold Cup at Newbury.

provided one of jumping's darkest ever moments, when he was caught close home by Dormant in the 1966 King George VI Chase at Kempton Park. 'Himself' had broken a pedal bone early in the race, finished crippled, and never ran again. At the time of his last race he was a few days short of his tenth birthday, in his prime as a chaser.

But of course the world of jump racing remembers Arkle not in defeat but in triumph:

- the effortless acceleration which took him past Mill House in that famous 1964 Gold Cup, and the sheer ease with which he beat the same horse out of sight in the 1965 running;
- his stroll round Cheltenham to win the 1966 Gold Cup despite his notorious blunder at the fence in front of the stands, which jockey Pat Taaffe explained by saying that Arkle was looking at the crowd;
- breaking Mill House's heart with a pulverising display to win the 1964 Hennessy, and his repeat win the following year;
- jumping spring-heeled round Sandown Park to land the 1965 Whitbread;
- and perhaps his greatest performance of all, giving Mill House 16lb and leaving that horse trailing in his wake in the 1965 Gallaher Gold Cup at Sandown Park, which has been described as the greatest display of sheer class in jump racing history.

Arkle's achievements were extraordinary, and his superiority to his contemporaries so complete that the precursor of the 'long handicap' system we know today was introduced in Ireland in 1964 to take account of his transcendence. Just think of that: he was so good that he changed the rules, and in any sporting sphere greatness does not come any bigger.

OPPOSITE: You can see why they called Mill House 'The Big Horse': Willie Robinson looks like a pea on a drum as they come in after winning the 1963 Hennessy Gold Cup. That was the only time that Mill House beat Arkle, as on four subsequent occasions 'Himself' proved his superiority beyond doubt. While it was Mill House's misfortune to be foaled in the same year as the greatest chaser of the lot, he left his own mark on jump racing, having won, in addition to the 1963 Hennessy, the Cheltenham Gold Cup and King George VI Chase the same year, and the 1967 Whitbread Gold Cup. Willie Robinson is one of a very select band of jockeys to have won the 'Big Three' jump races, having landed the Gold Cup on Mill House in 1963, Grand National on Team Spirit in 1964, and Champion Hurdle on Anzio in 1962 and Kirriemuir in 1965. (The other jockeys to have achieved that treble since the Second World War are Fred Winter, Bobby Beasley, Richard Dunwoody, Barry Geraghty and AP McCoy.) Willie also rode the runner-up in the Derby: 100-1 shot Paddy's Point, second to Hard Ridden in 1958.

But the appeal of Arkle went way beyond his feats on the racecourse, and the effect which he had on people has been well documented. There were poems and songs about him, and the daily flow of fan-mail with which the Dreaper yard was bombarded while the horse was in his prime became multiplied many times over in the wake of his career-ending injury. People's love of Arkle knew no bounds.

It has been said that he was the first great racehorse of the television age, the first equine superstar whose races could be followed live by a wide audience, and his exploits in the mid-1960s must have done jump racing the world of good.

Brough Scott was a young jump jockey when 'Himself' was climbing towards greatness, and his description of Arkle's first race at Cheltenham – indeed, his first race over fences – is worth quoting:

> *I remember exactly where I was when I first saw him: standing by the last fence at Cheltenham for the Honeybourne Novices' Chase on Saturday 17 November 1962. I was a nineteen-year-old amateur seriously affected by the racing bug and had no defence against the image in front of me. We had been warned the Irish thought this lean, greyhoundy long-eared thing was a bit special, but what happened at the finish just took the breath away. There were decent horses against him, but Arkle just skipped over the fence and sprinted twenty lengths clear as if he was another species altogether. Perhaps he was.*

Arkle was put down on 31 May 1970 at the age of 13 – a sadly premature end for the greatest of them all. His skeleton can be seen in the museum at the Irish National Stud in County Kildare, and his feats will live for ever.

Even when the true greatness of Arkle had become obvious, there were plenty who refused to consider him the equal of **Golden Miller**, owned by the extremely round, exceedingly rich and unbelievably eccentric Dorothy Paget (see page 61). One of the towering figures of jump racing in the twentieth century, she had many unusual habits, not the least of which was her daily – or nightly – routine. She tended to sleep through the day and get up for breakfast at 8.30pm, spending much of the night eating huge meals and phoning her long-suffering trainers. Paget was a punter on a scale to match all her other excesses, and with one of her bookmakers enjoyed a position of such trust that she would make bets in the evening on races that been run that afternoon!

In terms of pure record, you can see where those who place her beloved Golden Miller above Arkle in the all-time rankings are coming from. Golden Miller won the Gold Cup five years in a row

A record which may never be emulated: Golden Miller, ridden by Gerry Wilson, wins the 1934 Grand National to become the only horse to have won that race and the Cheltenham Gold Cup in the same year.

between 1932 and 1936 – no other horse has won more than three in a row – and remains the only horse ever to have won the Gold Cup and Grand National in the same year. He would probably have won the 1937 Gold Cup had it not been abandoned due to frost, and returned to Cheltenham at the age of eleven to finish runner-up to Morse Code in the 1938 Gold Cup – the only time he was ever beaten at Cheltenham.

Despite that 1934 Grand National win, Golden Miller seemed to hate Aintree, a fact which was yet to be heeded by punters when they sent him off at 2-1 for the 1935 National, the hottest favourite in the history of the race. In all he ran in the National five times, winning in 1934 but failing to get round on the other four occasions.

That was a different age, of course, when the Gold Cup was essentially a warm-up race for the Grand National, rather than the undisputed championship which it is today. But Golden Miller's Cheltenham record is surely one which will never be surpassed, and he deserves the recognition afforded by his statue gazing out over the parade ring from the grandstand.

In fact, he might well be looking at the paddock-side statue of **Dawn Run**, the great Irish mare with the unique record of having won both of Cheltenham's showpiece races, the Champion Hurdle and the Gold Cup.

I've already mentioned that it was seeing the amazing scenes which followed her Gold Cup victory under Jonjo O'Neill in 1986 which fired my love of Cheltenham and my ambition to succeed there, and I can never look at that statue without feeling again that first spark. It was an unbelievable performance by an unbelievable mare, and it produced one the greatest receptions in racing history.

In truth, Dawn Run was well behind the likes of Arkle or Golden Miller in terms of ability, but there was a sort of earthiness about

OPPOSITE: Great Champion Hurdlers. ABOVE, John Francome and Sea Pigeon – two legends in themselves – clear the last in pursuit of leaders Daring Run and Pollardstown before cruising up the Cheltenham hill to win the 1981 running. BELOW, See You Then, a spare ride for Steve Smith Eccles after John had been injured in the previous race, heads Gaye Brief before winning the first of his three Champion Hurdles in 1985. Steve rode him in all three – a dream chance ride!

Deep Run, sire of Dawn Run.

her which the jumping crowd loved – much as during the previous decade they had loved that street-fighter Red Rum.

And her background was hugely appealing. A daughter of the great jumping sire Deep Run, she was bred on a farm in County Cork and sold at auction for 5,800 guineas to Mrs Charmian Hill, a larger-than-life character, then 62 years old, who as Dawn Run grew up liked nothing better than to ride her mare, not only as part of her exercise at Paddy Mullins's yard but in races. 'The Galloping Granny' rode Dawn Run in her racecourse debut in a Clonmel bumper in May 1982, and two races later they won at Tralee – and Mrs Hill promptly hung up her riding boots.

Despite her unorthodox early career, Dawn Run started developing into a top-class racehorse. She was runner-up to Sabin du Loir in the Sun Alliance Novices' Hurdle at the Cheltenham Festival in 1983, then won a valuable novices' hurdle at Aintree and finished second to the then Champion Hurdler Gaye Brief the following day. By the time she beat Gaye Brief in the Christmas Hurdle at Kempton Park in December 1983 she was already a very live contender for the 1984 Champion Hurdle, a position strengthened by her winning the Irish Champion Hurdle at Leopardstown. At Cheltenham she was ridden by Jonjo O'Neill and, with Gaye Brief sidelined by injury, started odds-on favourite. She won narrowly, then went on to land the Grande Course de Haies at Auteuil, which made her the winner of the English, Irish and French Champion Hurdles.

Dawn Run graduated from hurdles to steeplechases for the 1984-85 season, but was afflicted by injury and ran only once that term, winning at Navan, and her build-up towards the 1986 Gold Cup was far from smooth. In her final prep race, at Cheltenham in January, she unseated her usual jockey Tony Mullins, who was replaced for the big day by Jonjo O'Neill.

The Gold Cup was only Dawn Run's fifth run over fences, but sometimes sheer determination – almost bloody-mindedness in her case – proves more important than experience, and so it proved. In a race I've described on pages 88–93, she rallied to catch Wayward Lad close home and set off scenes of delirium unparalleled even by Cheltenham standards.

That famous occasion was followed by anti-climax, when she fell at the first fence in the Whitbread Gold Label Cup at Aintree (nowadays the Totesport Bowl). She then won a match race – a head-to-head between two runners – against Queen Mother Champion Chase winner Buck House at Punchestown, and was sent to Auteuil again for a repeat win in the Grande Course de Haies. Ridden by French jockey Michel Chirol, she was prominent when at the fifth last she fell and broke her neck, dying instantly.

It was a terrible fate for a truly great horse – and I never forget that for me, it all really began with Dawn Run.

Dawn Run and Jonjo O'Neill immortalised in bronze at Cheltenham.

The fourth equine statue at Cheltenham – and the only one reproducing the horse life-size – brings us into the new millennium with **Best Mate**, winner of the Gold Cup in 2002, 2003 and 2004.

Owned by Jim Lewis, trained by Henrietta Knight and ridden to his three Gold Cup victories by Jim Culloty, Best Mate was a wonderful looking horse – bred in Ireland, though by the French stallion Un Desperado – whom Henrietta and her husband Terry Biddlecombe had discovered on the Irish point-to-point circuit. His first race in England came in 1999 in a Cheltenham bumper, which he won, and he moved on to become a high-class novice hurdler, finishing runner-up to Sausalito Bay in the Supreme Novices' Hurdle at the 2000 Cheltenham Festival before going on to win a valuable prize at Aintree.

In the 2000-01 season he was sent chasing and made a fine start, winning at Exeter, Cheltenham and Sandown Park before being

Best Mate and Jim Culloty coming back with Henrietta Knight and an emotional Terry Biddlecombe after winning their third Tote Cheltenham Gold Cup in 2004.

beaten at Aintree by another top-class prospect, Barton. The foot-and-mouth epidemic in spring 2001 removed his chance of winning one of the big novice chases at the Cheltenham Festival, but in March 2002 he arrived there as one of the better fancied horses in the Gold Cup.

His seventeen rivals included Florida Pearl, who had beaten Best Mate narrowly in the King George VI Chase the previous Christmas, and he started at 7-1 to take revenge – which he did with a tremendous surge up the straight and over the last two fences to win by a length and three quarters from Ted Walsh-trained Commanche Court.

After winning the Peterborough Chase at Huntingdon and the King George VI Chase (ridden by Tony McCoy), he returned to Cheltenham and, this time starting 13-8 favourite, netted a second Gold Cup, beating Truckers Tavern ten lengths.

By now there was a very clear pattern emerging. Best Mate was a true Premier League horse, and one who would not be asked to race unless it was absolutely necessary. He had had five runs in his first season, four in his second and third, and three in his fourth. Complaints that she was cosseting her star horse in cotton wool were water off a duck's back to Hen, and the justification of sticking to her guns came with the results. After being beaten by Jair du Cochet in the 2003 Peterborough Chase, Best Mate bypassed the King George at Christmas and went instead to Leopardstown, where he decisively beat Le Coudray to win the Ericsson Chase (now the Lexus).

Then to Cheltenham again, where he beat Sir Rembrandt by half a length to join the very select group of triple Gold Cup winners: Golden Miller, Arkle and Vincent O'Brien-trained Cottage Rake, who won the race in 1948, 1949 and 1950.

Best Mate was nine years old when he won his third Gold Cup, and the prospect of another was real enough. He started the 2004-05 campaign with a narrow victory over Seebald at Exeter and was beaten by Beef Or Salmon at Leopardstown – then injury ruled out the 2005 Gold Cup.

In November 2005 he made his seasonal debut in the William Hill Haldon Gold Cup at Exeter. Not a great deal was expected of him on his first run since the previous December, and it was no surprise that he was unable to stick with fitter horses (such as Kauto Star and the winner Monkerhostin) when the heat was turned on. He was pulled up early in the home straight, and as he was walking back dropped dead of a heart attack – a very sad end to a very fine horse.

I rode in all three of Best Mate's Gold Cups – out with the washing with Bacchanal in 2002, similarly remote on Marlborough in 2003, and pulled up on Irish Hussar in 2004 – so was able to enjoy a close-up view of his quality. He was a brilliant jumper and,

OPPOSITE: Oof! – but Richard Dunwoody sits tight on Desert Orchid and disaster is averted at the last fence of the Jameson Irish Grand National, 1990.

like so many of the great chasers, a horse with such a high cruising speed that in an ordinary race he tended to look like an ordinary horse – but the pace of a championship race brought out the champion in him.

OK, beating Truckers Tavern ten lengths or Sir Rembrandt half a length is not form of the calibre which suggests that Best Mate is on a par with Arkle. But a winner can only beat the horses who line up against him, and at his peak Best Mate was a superb horse.

Kempton Park, rather than Cheltenham, has a statue of **Desert Orchid**, which is entirely fitting, as Cheltenham never saw the great grey at his best – even when he won the 1989 Gold Cup, described on pages 93–6 – and Kempton did. He won the King George VI Chase no fewer than four times, a feat unmatched until Kauto Star notched the same tally (unlike Dessie, in four consecutive years) in 2009.

Everyone loved Dessie, and it's not difficult to work out why. His grey coat – which got significantly whiter as he got older – made him easy to follow in a race. But so did his usual style of racing, making the running with a rare flamboyance and jumping with a terrific zest and enthusiasm. That zest was apparent long after he had retired from racing. Year after year he would lead the parade for the King George VI Chase, usually ridden by his old comrade-in-arms Colin Brown, and after the runners had made their way to Kempton's three-mile start old Dessie would pull Colin's arms out as he careered past the stands, to the immeasurable delight of the Boxing Day crowd.

That rapture which Desert Orchid produced in those who witnessed his public appearances after he had stopped racing was much more than mere sentimentality. It was an expression of the very spirit of the sport, a joy at seeing how one of the all-time great horses retained all his enthusiasm.

Dessie raced only once in Ireland, when ridden by Richard Dunwoody to win the Irish National in 1990. He was English-bred, English-trained and English-owned, but the Irish turned out in droves to see him in the flesh. The fact that they wanted to be there to see a famous horse spoke volumes about the Irish attitude to horses, and volumes about the charismatic appeal of the great grey warrior.

Red Rum could trump all the above quintet, as he has not just one statue but two: at Aintree, where he posted his unique record of three wins in the Grand National, and at Ayr, where he won the Scottish Grand National in 1974 just two weeks after his second National victory. His Grand National record is given on page 161, but his massive popularity went far beyond what is preserved in the form book. He had overcome all sorts of problems in his early years and, having been bred for the Flat, his racing career had started when he was a two-year-old. The way in which this

Red Rum in his rightful place – out on his own at Aintree when winning his third National in 1977, Tommy Stack in the saddle.

indomitable horse – owned by Southport millionaire Noel Le Mare and trained by the then almost unknown Ginger McCain – rose to the status of national treasure summed up to perfection the idea that in jump racing, *anything* is possible.

As with Arkle (and indeed Dawn Run), there was a song about Red Rum, and he was the first racehorse to become an in-demand celebrity after he had stopped racing. While Arkle in his retirement had appeared for a week at the Horse of the Year Show, the post-racing Red Rum embarked on a fresh career as an equine celeb, and enjoyed a steady flow of nice little earners opening betting shops.

Where will there be a statue of **Kauto Star**? At Cheltenham, where the Paul Nicholls-trained favourite is the only horse ever to regain the Gold Cup title after losing it, or at Kempton Park, where he is the only horse to have won four consecutive runnings of the King George?

The story of his great rivalry with stable companion **Denman** – whose statue, wherever it is sited, should be made of granite rather than bronze – is summarised on pages 100–11.

Another famous grey ridden by Richard Dunwoody: One Man in January 1996 winning the King George VI Tripleprint Chase at Sandown Park, where the 1995 race was relocated after Kempton on Boxing Day had fallen victim to frost. One Man won a second King George at Kempton in December 2006. He also won the 1994 Hennessy Cognac Gold Cup at Newbury, and provided one of the great Cheltenham moments when, after twice failing in the Gold Cup, he won the 1998 Queen Mother Champion Chase. Tragically he was killed at Aintree on his next outing.

How about the jockeys?

Absolutely no surprise about where to start any list of the greatest riders in history: **AP McCoy** has raised the bar so high over the last decade and a half that he has brought a new dimension not only to jump racing itself, but to sporting achievement. What other major sport has been dominated by a single individual for so long?

Born in County Antrim, AP started to learn his trade with local trainer Billy Rock before going on to Jim Bolger, tutor to so many top-class jockeys and trainers. In summer 1994 he moved to England to join Toby Balding as conditional jockey, and won

FOLLOWING SPREAD: AP's greatest ride, driving the white-faced Wichita Lineman in pursuit of Nenuphar Collonges ('Choc' Thornton) before winning the William Hill Trophy at Cheltenham in 2008.

13

AP's second greatest ride, beating me in a camel race at Ascot in 2000.

the conditional jockeys' title for the 1994-95 season. The following season, his first as a fully fledged professional jockey, he won the jump jockeys' championship, and he has won it every year since – at the time of writing this, 15 consecutive seasons.

But as with any great sportsman, the facts tell only a small part of the story, and it is the character behind those facts which is so intriguing. For me – and for many others who have studied his extraordinary career at close quarters – the single word which sums AP up is 'determination'. It has been said of plenty of sporting heroes that they never know when they're beaten, but AP has taken that simple quality of determination to new heights: he is so totally focused on winning that losing simply does not enter the equation.

He's won pretty well all the big races, but there is no more graphic example of his never-give-up spirit than an extraordinary race at Southwell in January 2002. The Feast of St Raymond

Novices' Chase was by anybody's standards a minor affair, a humdrum entry in the champion jockey's diary, but what happened made it one of the most remarkable steeplechases I can remember.

AP was riding the odds-on favourite Family Business, trained by his then guv'nor Martin Pipe, in the seven-runner chase, and as they came into the straight with another circuit to go the field had already been reduced to five. At the middle fence in the straight Family Business jumped left and AP was unseated, much to his displeasure – he took off his helmet and hurled it to the ground as Family Business galloped off alone.

Then an increasing maelstrom of falling, remounting, unseating and refusing dogged the surviving four runners, to the point that after the fourth last fence, the final obstacle down the back, there were none left standing. Family Business had been caught on the far turn, and as soon as AP realised that, bizarrely, the race was still there to be won, he remounted his horse, went back to jump again the fence where he been unseated – which strictly he didn't need to do – and completed the race in his own time. (Immediately after AP had been dislodged, a punter on the betting exchange Betfair, who clearly underestimated our man's determination, had offered 1,000-1 against Family Business winning, and had two takers at £2 each!)

AP's comment afterwards was telling: 'I felt embarrassed at first because, basically, I fell off. But I don't mind how I win in the end – I'd be happy to win another like that in half an hour.'

Somehow that bizarre race sums up AP: complete focus ('I don't mind how I win in the end') and sheer determination allied to imagination, quick thinking, and a razor-sharp awareness of everything going on around him.

Of course, mental steel alone is not enough, and in harness with AP's strength of purpose goes the perfect physique. He is very, very strong, which underpins his extraordinary ability to get that extra

The Molony brothers, Tim (left) and Martin, two of the finest Irish jockeys of all. Tim was champion in Britain five times, and won the Cheltenham Gold Cup on Knock Hard in 1953 and four consecutive Champion Hurdles, on Hatton's Grace in 1951 and Sir Ken in 1952, 1953 and 1954. Martin rode much less in Britain than his brother, but won the 1951 Cheltenham Gold Cup on Silver Fame, plus several Irish Classics on the Flat – and was placed in both the Derby and Oaks at Epsom.

Stan Mellor, champion three times (1959-60, 1960-61 and 1961-2) and the first ever jump jockey to ride 1,000 winners, a tally he achieved in December 1971.

bit out of each and every runner, and his comparatively short legs and solid torso give him a very good centre of gravity which allows him to get right behind his horse and push, push, push.

While mental and physical strength obviously are hugely important in any successful jockey, jump racing has the added dimension of having to get your horse over the fences or hurdles, and the ability to 'see a stride' – that is, to telegraph to your horse the 'one, two, three, JUMP!' message which will take him smoothly over – is crucial. That is all about communication with your mount, which is the essence of true horsemanship, and AP has a great eye for a stride.

But it's not only AP who makes this a golden age of jump jockeys, and the style of **Ruby Walsh** forms a fascinating contrast with the champ's. While AP tells his horse what to do, Ruby's way is to ask – and consequently he's as wonderfully measured, sympathetic and stylish a rider as you could ever wish to see. Ruby has won the Gold Cup twice on Kauto Star and the Grand National on Papillon – trained by his father Ted – and Hedgehunter (see page 234) as well as countless other big races, and in 2010 he passed Pat Taaffe's record for most winners ridden at the Cheltenham Festival. In some ways it's remarkable that Pat's record stood for so long – he retired from the saddle in 1970 – and of course the meeting nowadays has more races than in his time, but Ruby's achievement is yet more evidence that he's the jockey any trainer or owner wants onside for the biggest races.

Dicky Johnson after winning the 2006 Greatwood Hurdle at Cheltenham on Detroit City.

And spare a thought for **Richard Johnson**, who is behind only AP in the list of winningmost jump jockeys but has never won the championship. In the 15 seasons that AP has been champion, Dicky has finished runner-up no fewer than twelve times. You won't hear him complaining, though.

AP's domination of riding over jumps is so comprehensive that the previous holder of the title, three-time champion **Richard**

Dunwoody, belongs to a different riding generation altogether. Richard was himself the king of the weighing room, a rider of rare quality who, like AP directly after him, brought race-riding to a fresh level. He was born to ride, and whatever he was doing on a horse – chasing or hurdling, racing, schooling or working – he did it with supreme style backed up by remarkable strength. And beyond that sublime horsemanship, he did his homework: he knew the form book inside out.

Ruby Walsh is unsurpassed at taking a horse over an obstacle – well illustrated by Denman at the Newbury water jump *en route* to landing the 2009 Hennessy Cognac Gold Cup.

We had our occasional differences, but for me Richard was simply a brilliant jockey, one of the best ever. His calm when landing the 1994 Grand National on Miinnehoma, a horse who simply could not be allowed to hit the front too soon, was a masterclass in coolness, and the fact that he was associated with so many great horses – among them Desert Orchid and One Man – is tribute to his exceptional skills.

I always thought **Peter Scudamore**, Richard's predecessor as champion, had rather a raw deal from riders in the stands, as his success was considered in some quarters to be more the result of head-down graft than of instinctive horsemanship,

A sight that has to be seen to be believed. Fred Winter gets the bitless Mandarin up to win the Grand Steeplechase de Paris in 1962 – a performance unsurprisingly voted the greatest ride ever by *Racing Post* readers.

and nothing could be further from the truth. Yes, Peter was not a man to throw in the towel prematurely – remember his extraordinary persistence when he kept pumping old Bonanza Boy along to stage a last-gasp victory in the 1989 Racing Post Chase? – but he was also a brilliant tactician and a rider of great sympathy when the horse required it. And like all the top jockeys of the modern era, he was a canny reader of the form book, well aware of what his opponents were capable of and the sort of race they might run.

Peter's career was closely linked with that of my great pal **John Francome**: so closely that when towards the end of the 1981–82

Peter Scudamore landing the 1993 Smurfit Champion Hurdle on Granville Again.

It's not only the big stars who ride the good horses. Mattie Batchelor, one of the hardest grafters but also the life and soul of the weighing room, wins the Sodexo Reynoldstown Novices' Chase at Ascot in 2009 on Carruthers.

season Scu, who had a long lead in the championship, broke a leg, John stopped riding for the season once he had drawn level.

John was as stylish a rider as you could ever wish to see, and what strikes me is how he has preserved his skill. Even now, in his mid-fifties, he'll go and school a few at Nicky Henderson's, and he looks as if he were thirty years younger. John in the saddle has always been poetry in motion. He'd never rush a horse, and try as you might, you'd never be able to detect the signals he's sending to his mount. For him, it all seemed – and seems – so effortless.

And by the way, it's not only the familiar jump jockeys who have left their mark on steeplechasing and hurdling, as plenty of jockeys famous for their exploits on the Flat have ridden under both codes. **Lester Piggott**, no less, rode twenty winners over hurdles between 1953 and 1959, including the 1954 Triumph Hurdle at Hurst Park on Prince Charlemagne. Four-time National Hunt champion **Josh Gifford** won the Manchester November Handicap and Chester Cup before moving to the jumps, while **Dave Dick** has the distinction of having been the only jockey ever to win both legs of the so-called Spring Double: the Lincoln Handicap on Gloaming in 1941, and Grand National on ESB in 1956. Much more recently, familiar names from the Flat like **Jamie Spencer**, **Richard Hughes** and **Johnny Murtagh** have ridden at the Cheltenham Festival. And don't forget that the first ever winner for Flat champion **Ryan Moore** was over hurdles at Towcester.

This is going to be some party: Paul Carberry coming back after winning the 1999 Martell Grand National on Bobbyjo. Paul's father Tommy Carberry won two Cheltenham Gold Cups and the National on L'Escargot, plus another Gold Cup on Ten Up, while his brother Philip won the 2007 Champion Hurdle on Sublimity, and his sister Nina is one of the leading lady jockeys.

Moving on to the major owners, let's go back to statues …

Sandown Park has a life-size equine bronze of a horse, one hardly within touching distance of Arkle, Golden Miller or Best Mate in terms of sheer ability but none the less a chaser with very close links to the course, and to the most popular owner in jump racing history. Special Cargo won the Grand Military Gold Cup at Sandown three times but is best remembered for his astonishing victory in the 1984 Whitbread Gold Cup, a famous race described on page 47. And Special Cargo was owned by **Her Majesty Queen Elizabeth the Queen Mother**.

The Queen Mother, who died in March 2002 at the age of 101, was the best supporter the sport could ever have had, and it is impossible to calculate the benefit that all involved in jumping have gained from her participation. She was loved by every true follower of jump racing, and she had a very special place in my affections, as I rode for her often after Nicky Henderson had become her principal trainer, following in the footsteps of legends Peter Cazalet and Fulke Walwyn.

A photo which always brings a smile to my face: Nicky Henderson and I with the Queen Mother.

In addition to Special Cargo and Devon Loch, who wrote his name in jumping history in the most unfortunate manner imaginable (see pages 177–9), a string of very successful horses bore the Queen Mother's colours of 'blue, buff stripes, blue sleeves, black cap, gold tassel'. There were top chasers like Manicou, who won the 1950 King George VI Chase (named after her husband), The Rip, Laffy, Double Star, Black Magic, Inch Arran, Isle Of Man, Sunyboy, The Argonaut and – perhaps the best of them all – Game Spirit. And there were fine hurdlers like Makaldar and Tammuz.

Even though I'm Irish, I always felt a foot taller when riding for the Queen Mother – and I wasn't the only jockey who made sure he had a clean pair of breeches before putting on those famous colours. There was an extra buzz when riding for her, and I'm sure that a factor in that feeling was that she was a true lover of the sport, as happy to be at Fontwell or Plumpton on a rainy Tuesday as in the royal box at some grander occasion.

I rode her very last winner, three weeks before she died: First Love in a novices' hurdle at – where else? – Sandown Park, where there is not only a statue of Special Cargo, but a bust of the Queen Mother herself. (Along with the Queen Mother's other horses, First Love subsequently ran in the colours of the Queen, who had not owned jumpers since taking over her father's flat horses when she acceded to the throne in 1952.) Her death left an immense gap in jumping, but her racing life ensured a rich legacy of wonderful memories.

If the Queen Mother gave the stamp of royal approval to jump racing, **JP McManus** is racing royalty in his own right, and I'm proud to have ridden a good few winners in his famous green and gold silks, which over the years have become synonymous with the Cheltenham Festival.

Anne, Duchess of Westminster, the face behind the yellow, black hoop, black cap with gold tassel, colours immortalised by Arkle.

Gratifyingly for one who has put such a huge amount into the sport, JP has enjoyed a fair measure of Festival success, notably with triple Champion Hurdle winner Istabraq, and more recently when Binocular landed the same race in 2010 – and in 2009 he owned the first three home in the Glenfarclas Cross-Country Chase, a remarkable result. And his long quest to own the Grand National winner has been finally rewarded with the victory of AP and Don't Push It.

But while JP is a gracious winner, he's also a fantastic loser – and the same can't necessarily be said about all owners! He's completely genuine in his passion for the sport, and has nothing but his horses' interests at heart: witness how he loves to retire his old warriors to the paddocks around his house in Ireland.

The Queen Mother with her racing manager Sir Michael Oswald (left) and Nicky Henderson after Bella Macrae had won at Sandown Park in 2001.

JP McManus having a chat with his three-time Champion Hurdle winner Istabraq, enjoying a happy retirement.

As a measure of the influence which JP McManus has had on jump racing, just imagine what the sport would have been like without his involvement.

The history of jump racing has been graced with dozens of top-class trainers, and from a jockey's point of view the quality he most wants to see in any trainer – from the legends of the sport to the humblest permit-holder – is an ability to get a horse fit enough to win a race. It's as simple as that.

But what sets the best trainers apart from the lesser operators is the ability to do that with great regularity, and to get a mediocre horse to perform better than his previous form suggests he will.

For me, it's highly significant that two of the greatest Flat trainers have also made their mark over the jumps.

Vincent O'Brien, who died in 2009, had an astonishing record over jumps before concentrating his attention on the Flat from the late 1950s, a career that saw a steady succession of great horses such as Sir Ivor and Nijinsky pass through his expert hands. He won the Cheltenham Gold Cup four times – with Cottage Rake in 1948, 1949 and 1950 and Knock Hard in 1953 – and the Champion Hurdle three times, with Hatton's Grace in 1949, 1950 and 1951, but perhaps his finest achievement as a jumps trainer was winning three consecutive Grand Nationals with three different horses – Early Mist in 1953, Royal Tan in 1954, Quare Times in 1955 – a feat never matched. On a slightly less elevated level, but arguably even more remarkable, is that between 1952 and 1959 he had twelve runners in divisions of the Gloucestershire Hurdle – now the Supreme Novices' Hurdle – at the Cheltenham National Hunt Meeting (as the Festival was then called), and ten of them won, with the other two both runners-up.

David Nicholson with his great two-mile chaser Viking Flagship. A fine jump jockey (he won the 1967 Whitbread Gold Cup on Mill House), 'The Duke' excelled as a trainer, winning the championship in the 1993–94 and 1994–95 seasons, and many big races, notably the Cheltenham Gold Cup with Charter Party in 1988, the Queen Mother Champion Chase with Viking Flagship in 1994 and 1995, and the King George VI Chase with Barton Bank in 1993.

AND
REFRESHMENTS

Two greats: Fred Winter and John Francome on the Lambourn gallops.

Aidan O'Brien is no relation to Vincent, but has the same instinctive feel for a horse – and in particular what is going on in that horse's brain – which is characteristic of all the truly great trainers, Flat or jumps. Among his many big-race wins over jumps, he won three consecutive Champion Hurdles with Istabraq in 1998, 1999 and 2000, and the 1996 Whitbread Gold Cup with Life Of A Lord.

Like both O'Briens, the trio of dominant jumping trainers a generation or so ago had ridden in races.

Fred Winter was one of the all-time great jump jockeys, champion four times in the 1950s; winning rider in two Grand Nationals, two Cheltenham Gold Cups, three Champion Hurdles and three runnings of the King George VI Chase; and human hero of that amazing race in 1962, when he steered the bitless Mandarin round the twists and turns of Auteuil to win the Grand Steeplechase de Paris. (see page 216) He's the only man to have both ridden and trained the winners of jump racing's three biggest prizes:

- **Grand National**: rode Sundew (1957) and Kilmore (1962); trained Jay Trump (1965 – his very first season with a licence) and Anglo (1966);
- **Cheltenham Gold Cup**: rode Saffron Tartan (1961) and Mandarin (1962); trained Midnight Court (1978);
- **Champion Hurdle**: rode Clair Soleil (1955), Fare Time (1959), and Eborneezer (1961); trained Bula (1971 and 1972), Lanzarote (1974) and Celtic Shot (1988).

PREVIOUS SPREAD: Vincent O'Brien (in trilby hat, to the left of the white-faced police horse on the right) coming in with winner Early Mist (Bryan Marshall) after the 1953 Grand National.

Among a stream of horses to have benefited from the Winter magic were Crisp, whose finest (and saddest) hour is described on pages 181-85; Pendil, twice winner of the King George VI Chase and beaten a short head by The Dikler in the 1973 Gold Cup; and the brilliant novice chaser Killiney, sadly killed in a fall at Ascot a few days after Crisp's Grand National.

And it wasn't only the handling of equine talent at which he excelled: John Francome spent his entire riding career at Fred's Lambourn yard.

If you don't consider Fred Winter a 24-carat hero, you're following the wrong sport.

Over the wall from Fred's Uplands yard is Saxon House, for so long the headquarters of his great friend and training rival **Fulke Walwyn**. Fulke had ridden Golden Miller late in that great horse's career and won the 1936 Grand National as an amateur jockey on Reynoldstown, after which he turned professional. He switched to training following a fall at Ludlow had left him unconscious for a month, and on the death of Peter Cazalet in 1973 took over as trainer for the Queen Mother, with whom he enjoyed a long and highly successful association.

Like Fred Winter, Fulke's training record was phenomenal. He was champion trainer five times, and his tally in the 'Big Three' reads:

- **Cheltenham Gold Cup**: four wins: Mont Tremblant (1952), Mandarin (1962), Mill House (1963) and The Dikler (1973);
- **Champion Hurdle**: two wins: Anzio (1962) and Kirriemuir (1965);
- **Grand National**: one win: Team Spirit (1964).

In addition, he won the King George VI Chase five times, Whitbread Gold Cup seven times, Hennessy Gold Cup seven times, and that fabled 1962 Grand Steeplechase de Paris with Mandarin.

Fred Rimell, who was champion jump jockey four times and won the Champion Hurdle on Brains Trust in 1945, took out his

Two more greats: Fulke Walwyn and Mandarin.

FOLLOWING SPREAD: Michael Dickinson with 'The Famous Five', the first five home in the 1983 Cheltenham Gold Cup. Left to right: Ashley House (fifth), Silver Buck (fourth), Wayward Lad (third), Captain John (runner-up) and winner Bregawn. Michael hardly looks old enough to be training Gold Cup runners ...

I'd like to know what these two are thinking: Martin and David Pipe on the Nicholashayne gallops.

'One man, Doumen!' Francois Doumen has added an extra dimension to jump racing with his regular French raiders in the big British races, an initiative which has been crowned with great success through horses like Nupsala (King George VI Chase in 1987); The Fellow (Cheltenham Gold Cup in 1994 and King George in 1991 and 1992); Algan (King George 1994); First Gold (King George 2000); and Baracouda (Stayers' Hurdle at Cheltenham 2002 and 2003).

first training licence that year, and has the unique distinction of winning four Grand Nationals with four different horses. His record in jumping's Triple Peaks is:

- **Cheltenham Gold Cup**: two wins: Woodland Venture (1967) and Royal Frolic (1976);
- **Champion Hurdle**: two wins: Comedy Of Errors (1973 and 1975);
- **Grand National**: four wins: ESB (1956), Nicolaus Silver (1961), Gay Trip (1970) and Rag Trade (1976).

In more recent times, **Martin Pipe** has seemed to break the mould of training horses to race over jumps. He has achieved this not only through his well-publicised exercise regime of working his horses in the equine equivalent of interval training – working up a steep gallop, then walking down, then going up the gallop again, as many times as is appropriate for that stage in the horse's fitness plan – but through paying close attention to such factors as blood-testing and the chemical balance of the horse's metabolism. Beyond all that, Martin – who handed over the reins to his son David in 2006 – is scrupulously logical in his thinking, and a very canny reader of both the form book and the programme book.

He could be very precise in his pre-race instructions, which were always worth listening to. I remember riding a good horse of his named Catch The Cross in a conditional jockeys' hurdle at Bangor, when his instructions were: 'Drop in, creep round don't take it up before the last – and I mean don't take it up before the last – and he'll win.' I did as he ordered, and we won – but only just, as Catch The Cross was one of those horses who stop the moment they hit the front, and halfway up the short Bangor run-in, while cutting things fine, was almost too early for him to get his nose in front.

Paul Nicholls with the brightest of his many stable stars: Kauto Star (left) and Denman.

It is a tribute to Martin's skills that he was champion trainer so many times – every year from the 1988–89 season to the 2004–05 season, apart from two seasons when David Nicholson had the top spot – and testament to his influence that so many other trainers cottoned on to how he was going about getting the very best out of every horse in his care. Some horses couldn't cope with the Pipe routine, but those who could would arrive at the racecourse fit to run for their lives.

Martin's supremacy of his trade could not last for ever, and it has been no surprise to me that his successor at the summit is **Paul**

Nicholls, for whom I rode many big-race winners, including See More Business in the Gold Cup and Call Equiname in the Queen Mother Champion Chase. Himself a successful jump jockey, Paul started small as a trainer: I can remember when he had just three horses in his care, but already there was the passion, the focus and the concentration that took him to the very top.

His domination of the training ranks has rivalled that of Martin Pipe immediately before him, and the top-class horses he's had in his care is just staggering, including Kauto Star and Denman, of course, plus another Gold Cup winner in the form of See More Business. When I won the King George VI Chase on See More Business in 1999, I could scarcely believe how Paul had freshened the horse up after he'd had a very hard race in the Charlie Hall Chase at Wetherby.

I am a huge admirer of Paul, and of his fellow West Country resident **Philip Hobbs** – trainer of such hugely popular horses as

Three of the greats. On the left, Sir Peter O'Sullevan, one of my all-time racing heroes, whose voice has always for me been the soundtrack of the sport – and I'm proud to have ridden a few winners in his colours (see pages 131-2). In the centre is Ginger McCain, trainer of the immortal Red Rum and a fourth National winner in Amberleigh House (2004). And on the right is Jenny Pitman, first lady to train a Cheltenham Gold Cup winner (Burrough Hill Lad in 1984, followed up with Garrison Savannah in 1991) and first lady to train a Grand National winner (Corbiere in 1983 – followed up with Royal Athlete in 1995).

Behind every top trainer is a great team. Albert 'Corky' Browne, Nicky Henderson's head lad, has been with the Henderson team since the beginning, and Nicky would not have achieved what he has without Corky and his like.

2003 Champion Hurdle winner Rooster Booster and that ageless chaser Monkerhostin – but of the present generation of trainers, I naturally have to pay special tribute to **Nicky Henderson**, for whom I rode as stable jockey for so many years. Seven Barrows, the historic yard just outside Lambourn which he took over from Peter Walwyn, is a wonderful place to be, and I so miss being there every morning to ride out, work or school.

At the root of Nicky's success is an obvious but crucial fact: he absolutely loves his horses. He's a complete gentleman, as brilliant a loser as a winner, and he can be very emotional – as you would expect from a man so close to the incumbents of his stable. He's a genius at spotting talent in a horse and then nurturing that talent to bring the individual to his full potential, unsurpassed at bringing the horse along at a rate with which that individual is comfortable. He has a superb eye for detail (which is common to all the truly great trainers) and a knack at PR (which is not).

Of course, Nicky is fortunate that his owners – which include Her Majesty the Queen, JP McManus, Sir Robert Ogden and the

John Oaksey with Mattie Batchelor after another win by Carruthers, the top chaser bred and co-owned by John. In his younger days John Lawrence – as he was before inheriting his father's title Lord Oaksey – was a notable amateur rider, winning the 1958 Whitbread and Hennessy Gold Cups on Taxidermist and just getting beaten on Carrickbeg in the 1963 Grand National. But everyone in racing owes him an unpayable debt for his part in the founding of the Injured Jockeys' Fund in the 1960s. It was the determination of John and a few like-minded friends which created the IJF, which has been a lifeline – literally, in some cases – for so many jockeys.

Lloyd Webbers – are the sort who will not want a horse's well-being put in jeopardy in order to rattle off a few wins and have that greatest virtue that an owner can possess: patience. He's also fortunate in his staff, many of whom – like head lad Corky Browne and travelling head lad Johnny Worrall (who announced his retirement in 2010) – have been with him for decades, and his relationship with his staff is built on complete trust.

For all the blue-bloods – equine and human – at a place like Seven Barrows, the real romance of jump racing is that at its highest level it embraces both the very big operations and the very small. There's no better illustration of that than the 1990 Gold Cup, when **Sirrell Griffiths**, a dairy farmer from near Carmarthen, drove the horsebox carrying Norton's Coin – one of only three horses he trained – to Cheltenham to win the jumping's most prestigious prize at 100-1, beating the legendary Desert Orchid into third place.

An engrossing sport full of ups and downs, thrills and spills, colour, noise and excitement, whose heroes and heroines include a dairy farmer and the Queen Mother as well as Arkle and Dawn Run – that's the wonderful world of jump racing.

OPPOSITE: Hedgehunter – ridden by Ruby Walsh and trained by Willie Mullins (on the right) – being led in by owner Trevor Hemmings after winning the 2005 John Smith's Grand National. Trevor has been one of the great supporters of jump racing – I'm delighted to have ridden many winners for him, including Trabolgan in the 2005 Hennessy – and has always been one of the sport's true gentlemen. Winning the National was one of his proudest days.

INDEX

Page numbers in *italics* refer to illustration captions.